NOTE-FOR-NOTE
KEYBOARD
TRANSCRIPTIONS

JAZZ
STANDARDS

MW00667347

ISBN 978-1-4234-3851-9

HAL•LEONARD®
CORPORATION
7777 W. BLUEMOUND RD. P.O. BOX 13819 MILWAUKEE, WI 53213

Visit Hal Leonard Online at
www.halleonard.com

CONTENTS

Blue and Sentimental

Words and Music by Jerry Livingston, Count Basie and Mack David

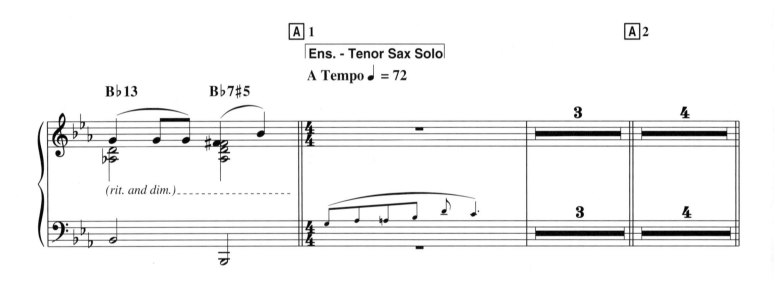

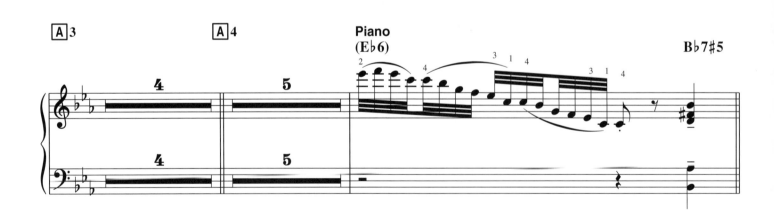

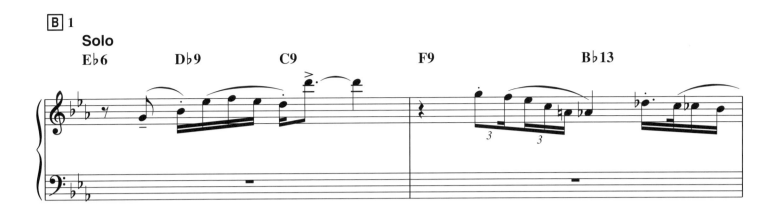

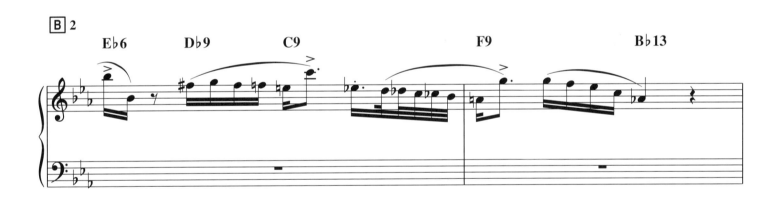

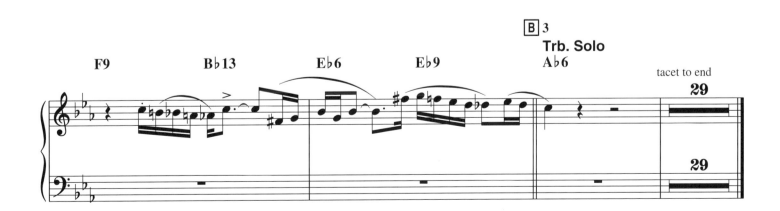

Blue Skies

from *BETSY*

Words and Music by Irving Berlin

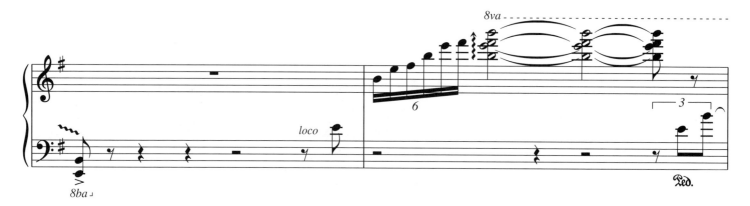

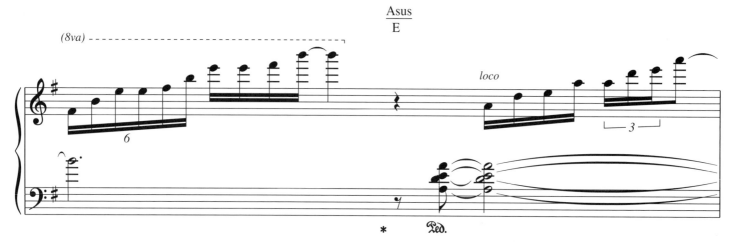

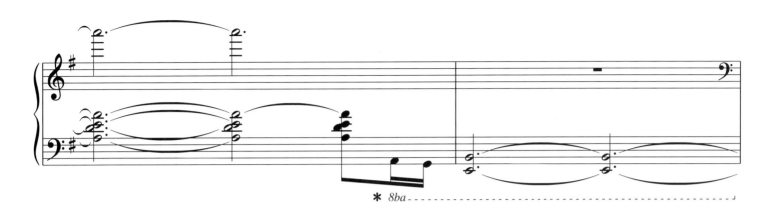

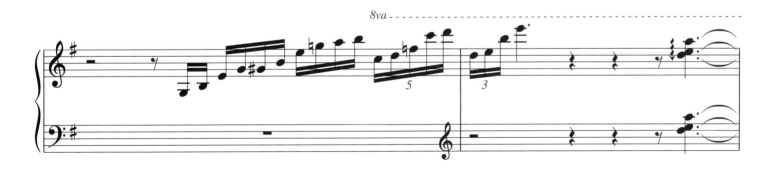

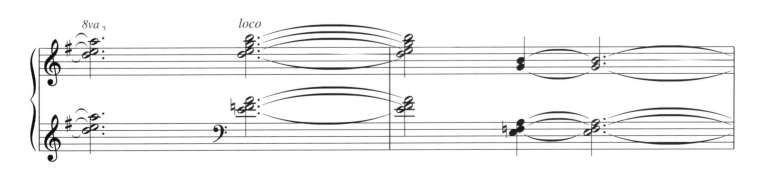

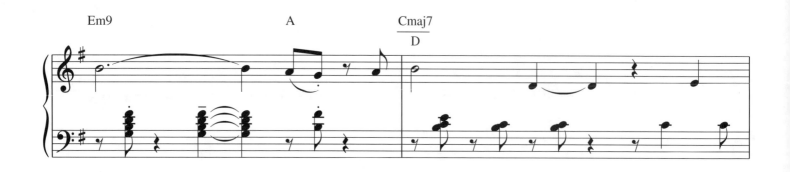

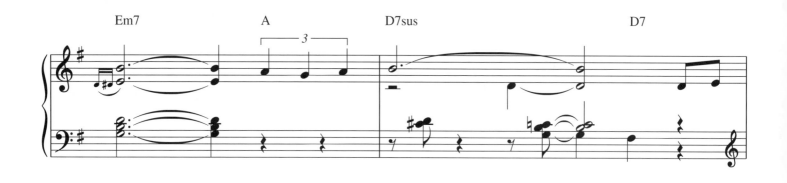

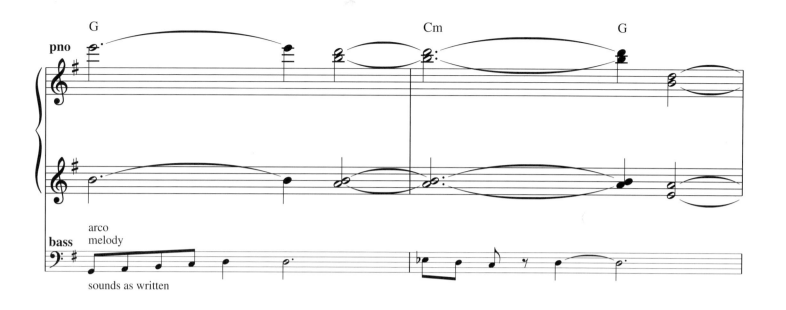

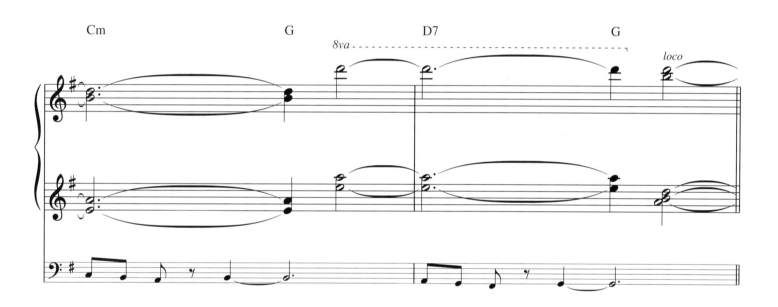

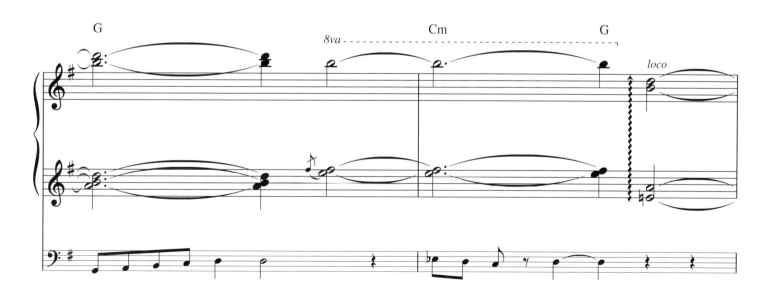

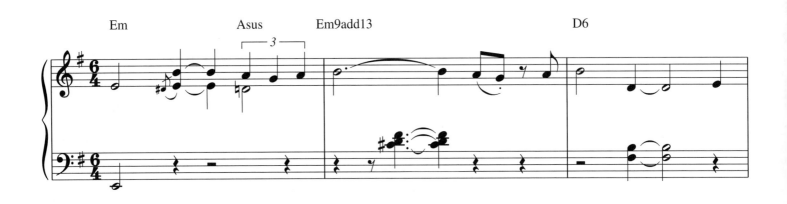

Bass Solo

Piano Solo

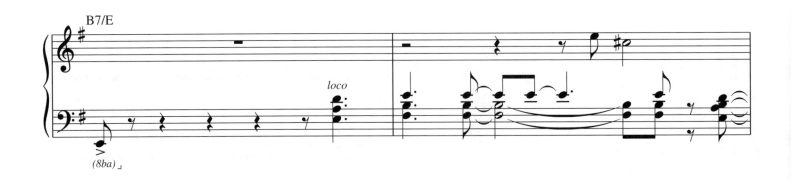

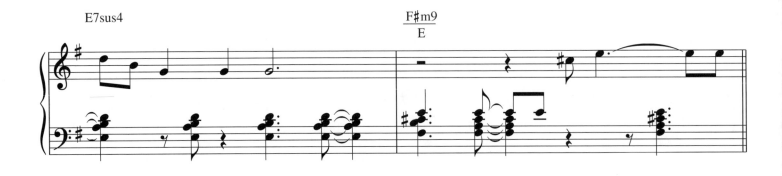

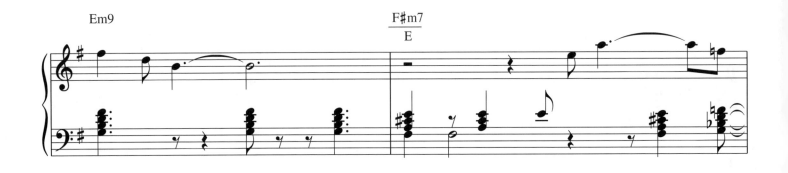

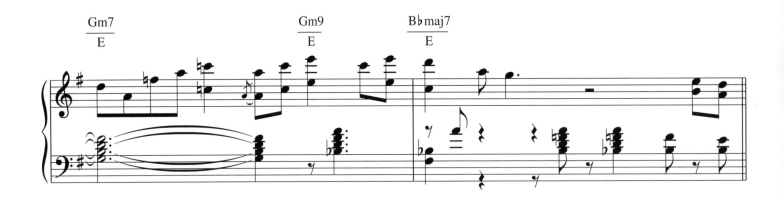

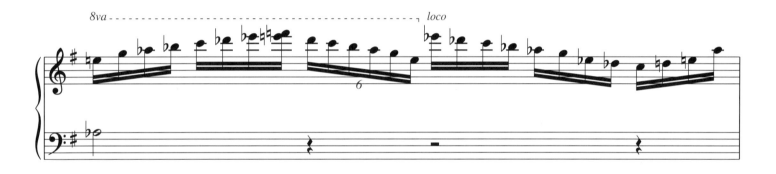

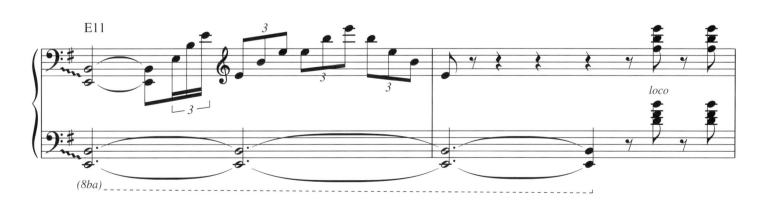

13

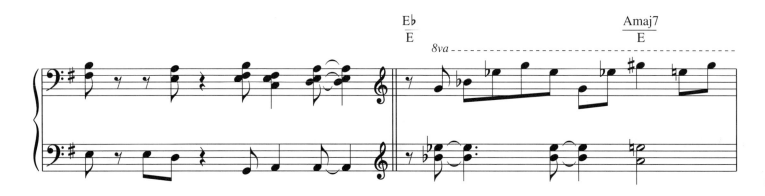

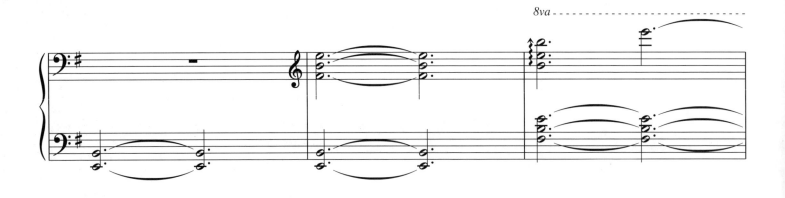

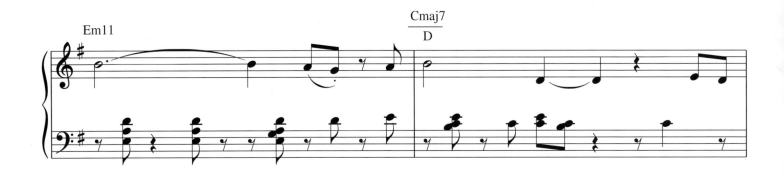

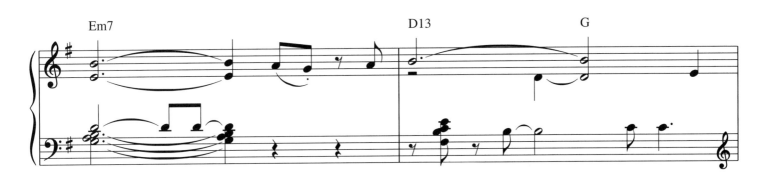

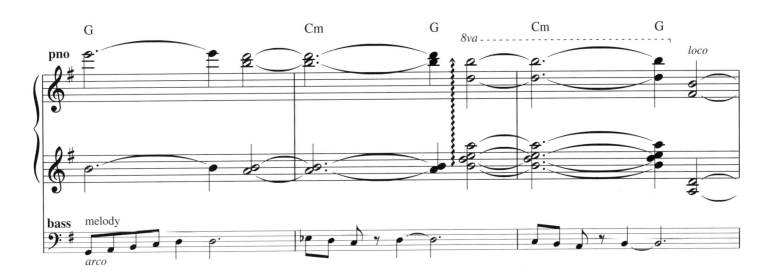

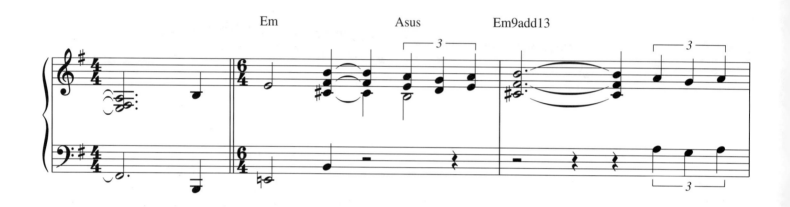

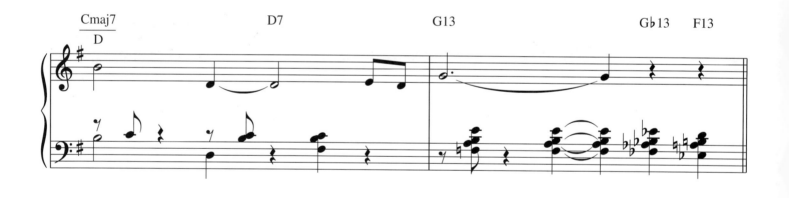

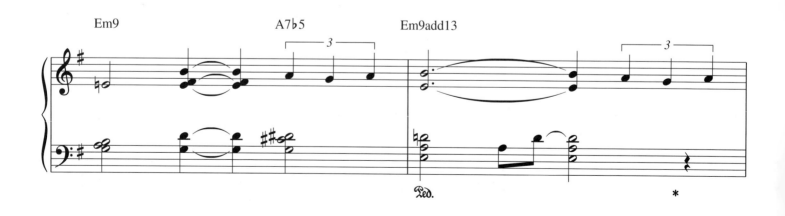

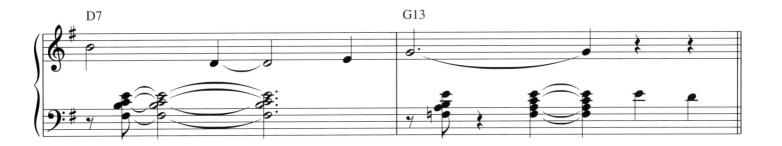

All the Things You Are

from *VERY WARM FOR MAY*

Lyrics by Oscar Hammerstein II
Music by Jerome Kern

♩ = 150

Quasi rubato, straight eighths

(Left hand only until indicated)

♩ = 130 **Slower, non rubato**

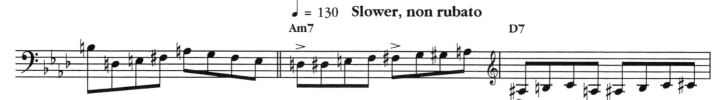

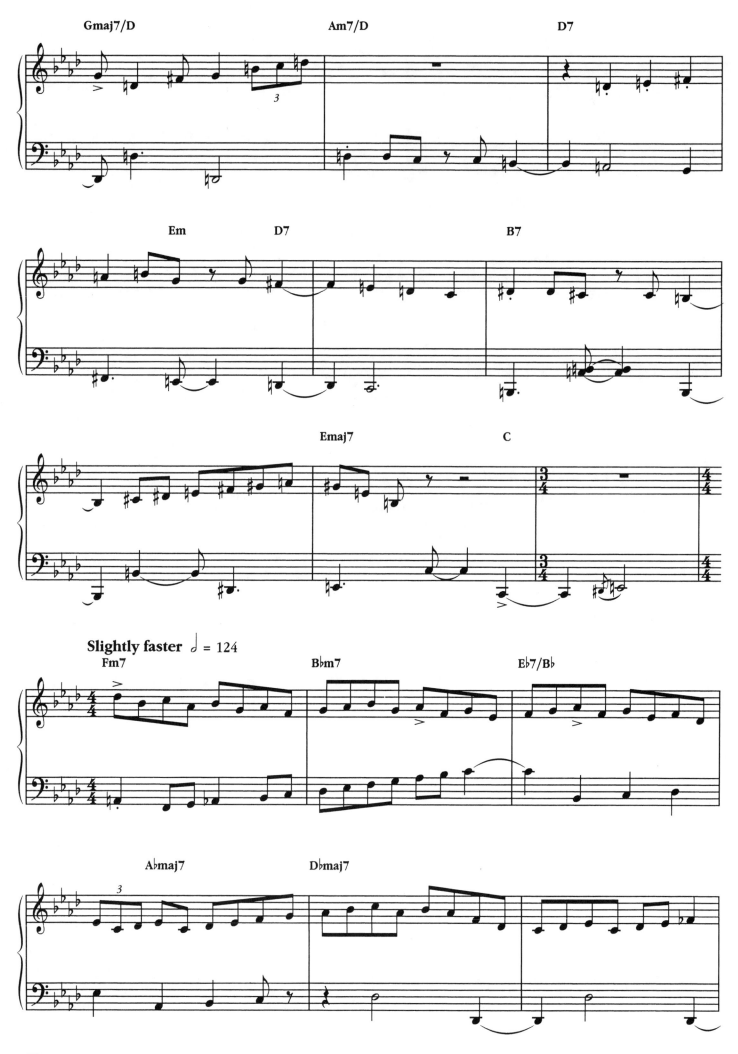

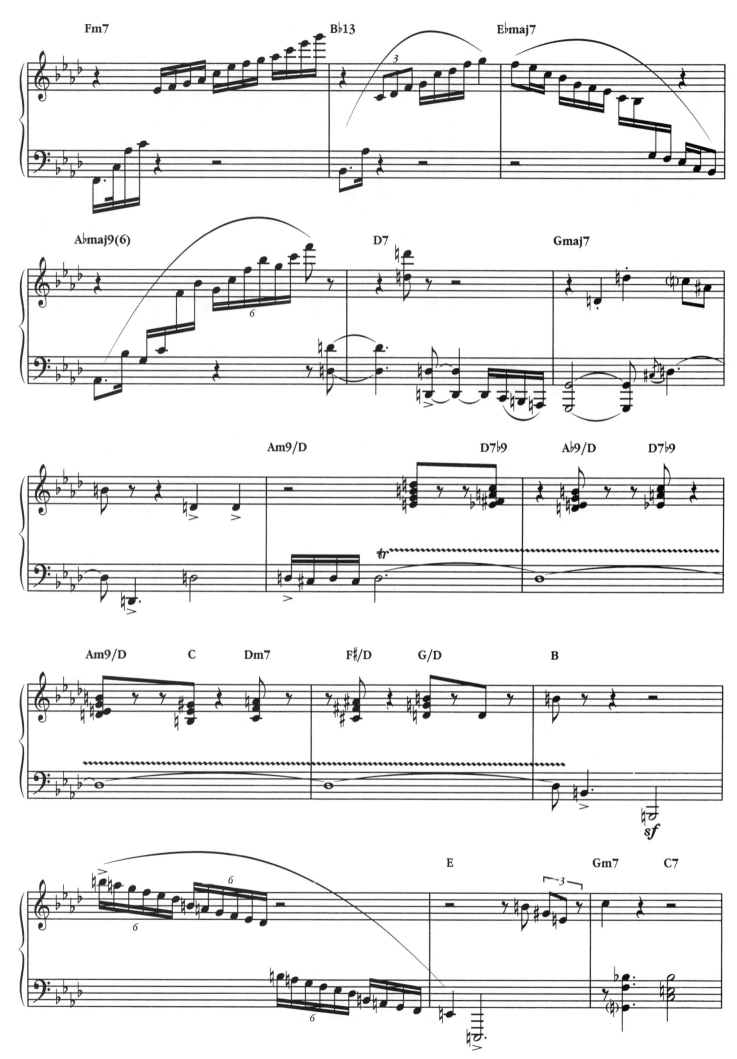

Caravan

from *SOPHISTICATED LADIES*

Words and Music by Duke Ellington, Irving Mills and Juan Tizol

1st Chorus

2nd Chorus

Come Rain or Come Shine

from *ST. LOUIS WOMAN*

Words by Johnny Mercer
Music by Harold Arlen

$\quad \quad = 86$

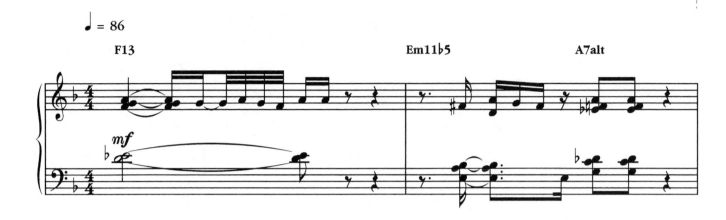

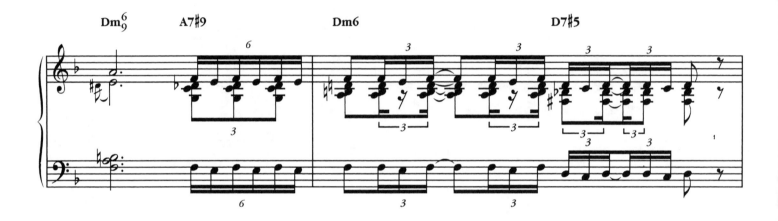

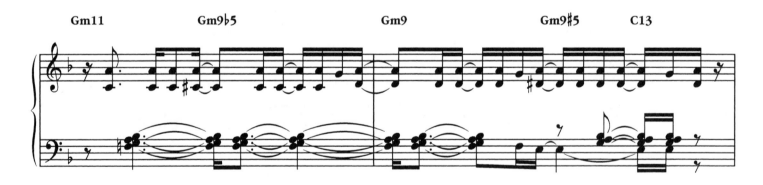

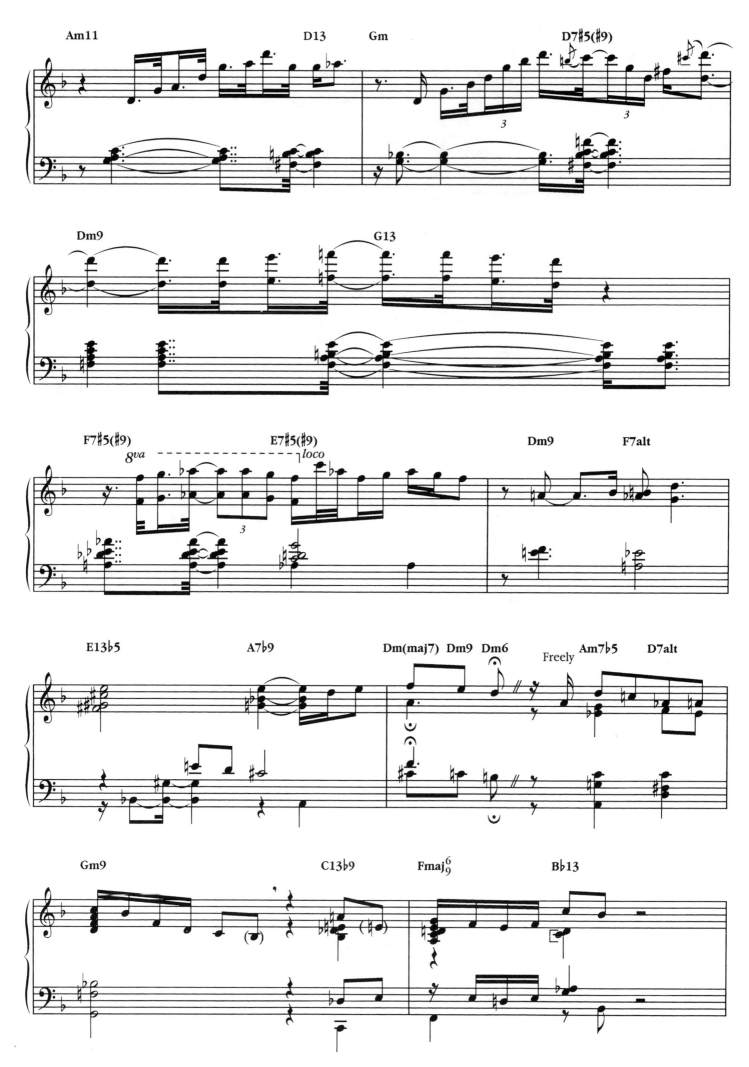

Don't Blame Me

Words by Dorothy Fields
Music by Jimmy McHugh

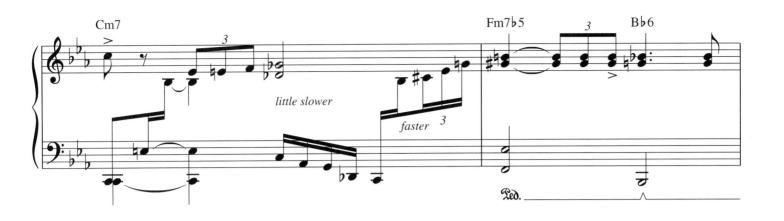

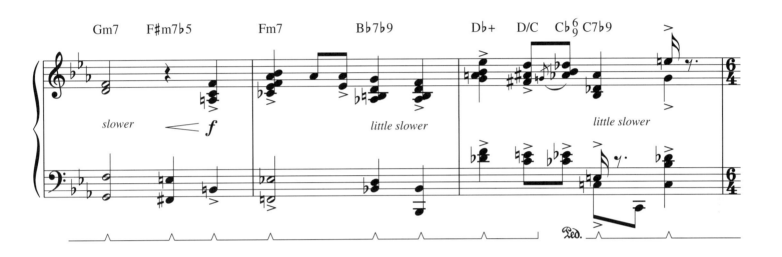

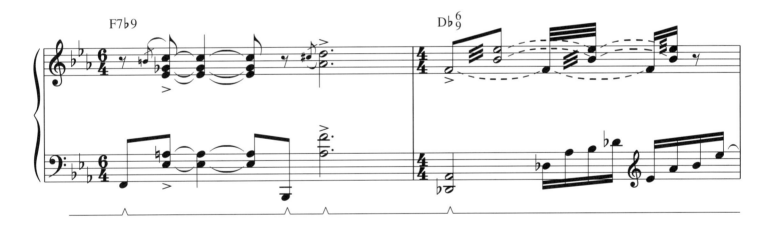

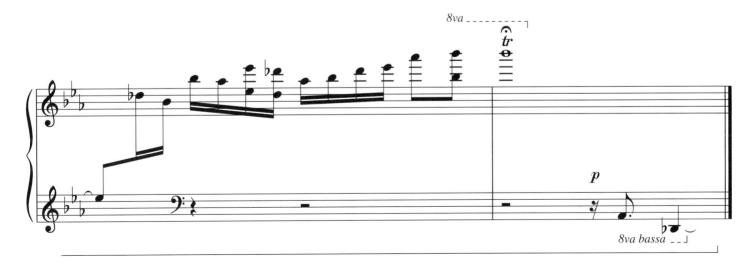

The Folks Who Live on the Hill

from *HIGH, WIDE AND HANDSOME*

Lyrics by Oscar Hammerstein II
Music by Jerome Kern

Honeysuckle Rose

from *AIN'T MISBEHAVIN'*

Words by Andy Razaf
Music by Thomas "Fats" Waller

Andante (♩ = 92)

*Grace note on the beat.

I Can't Stop Loving You

Words and Music by Don Gibson

I Remember You

from the Paramount Picture *THE FLEET'S IN*

Words by Johnny Mercer
Music by Victor Schertzinger

I'm Old Fashioned

from *YOU WERE NEVER LOVELIER*

Words by Johnny Mercer
Music by Jerome Kern

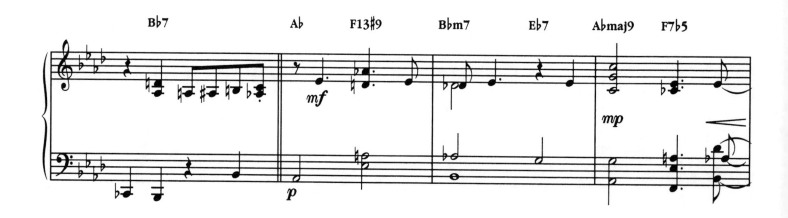

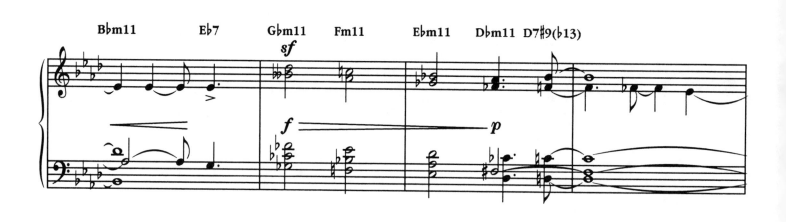

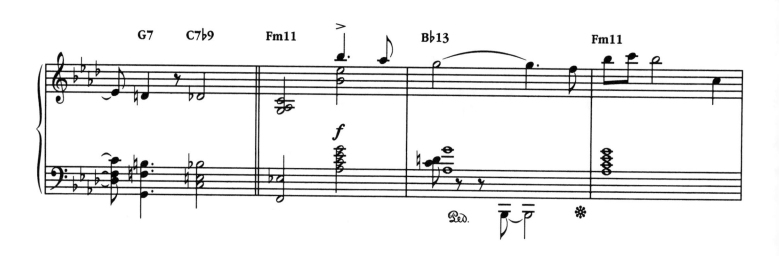

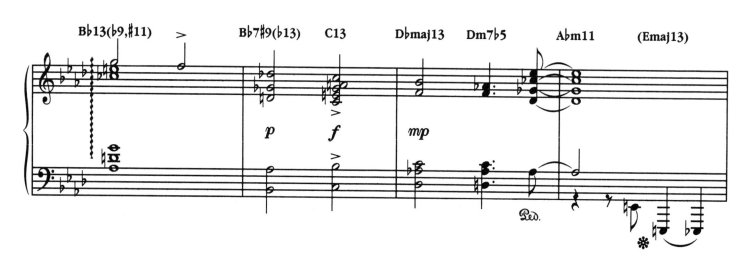

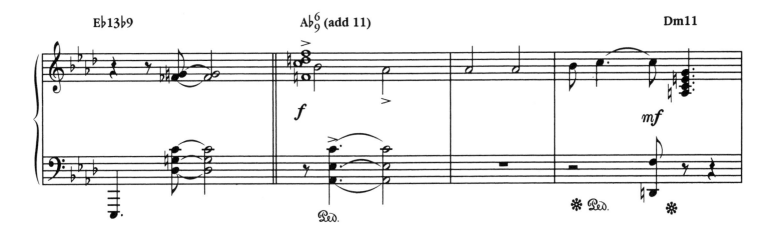

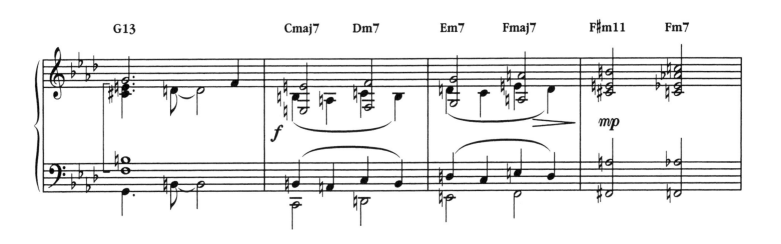

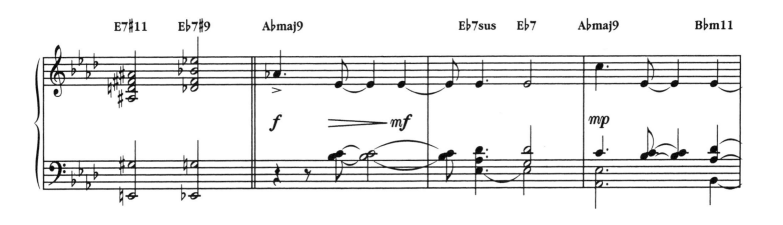

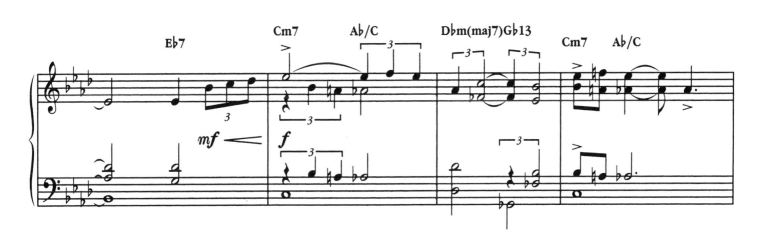

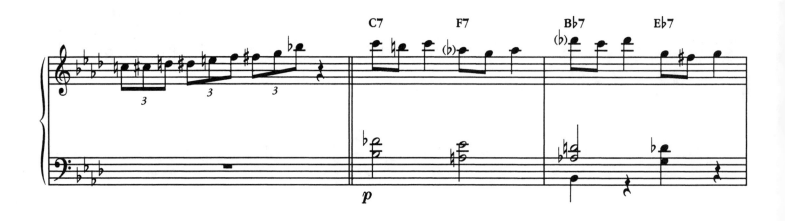

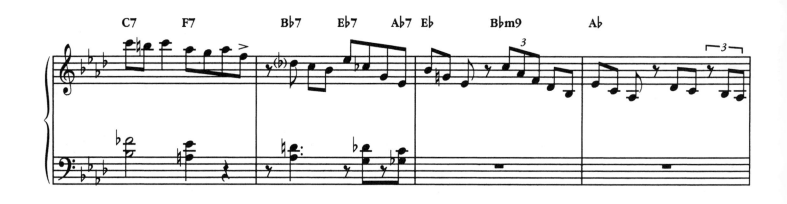

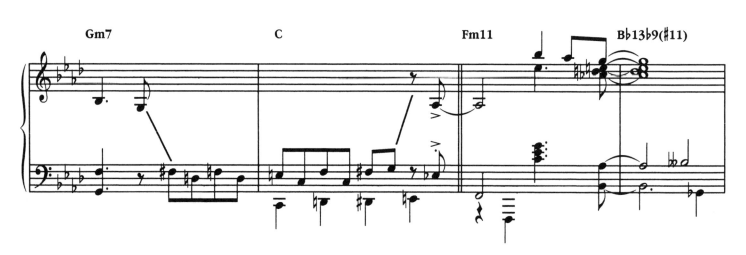

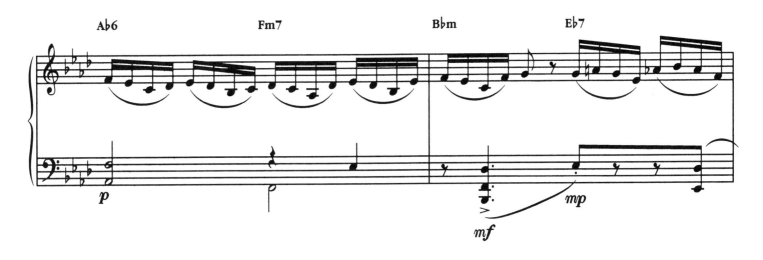

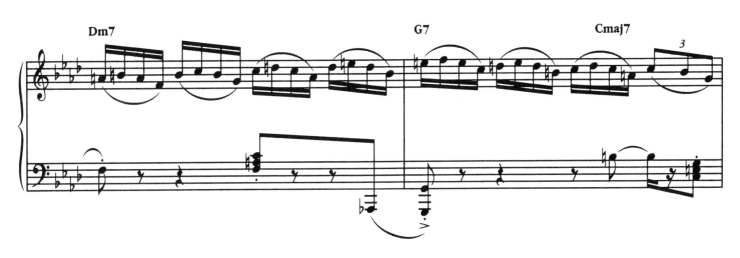

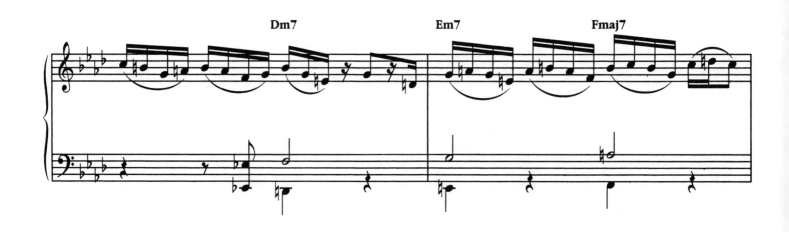

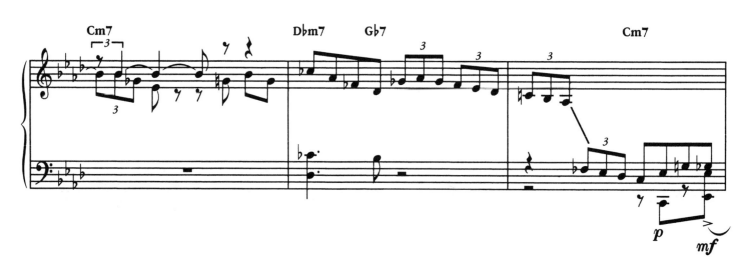

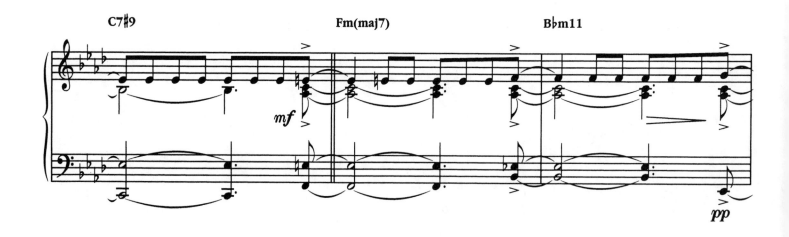

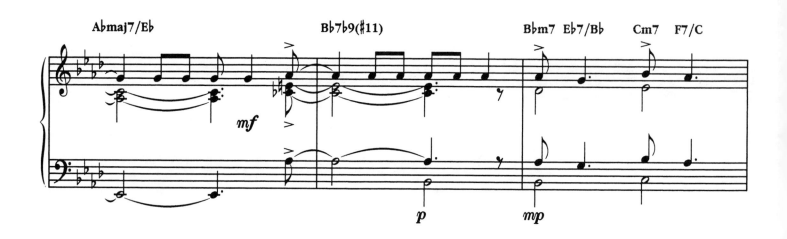

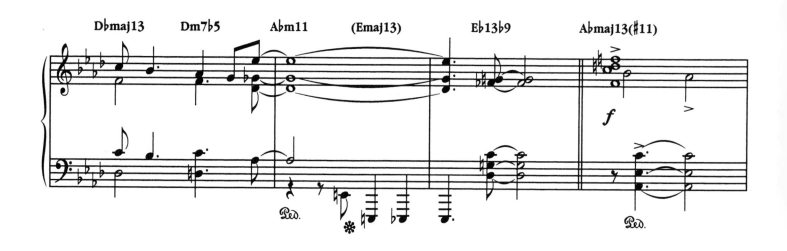

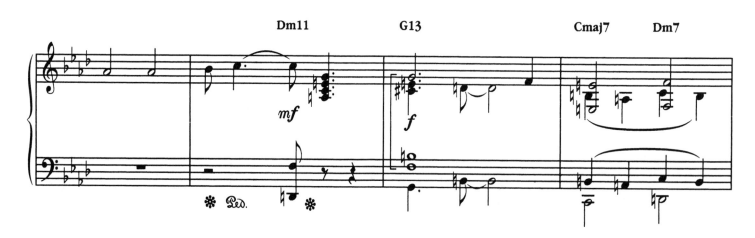

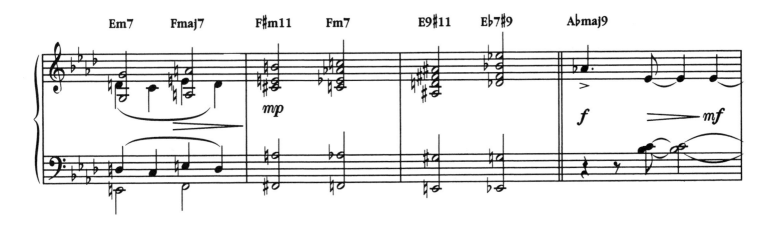

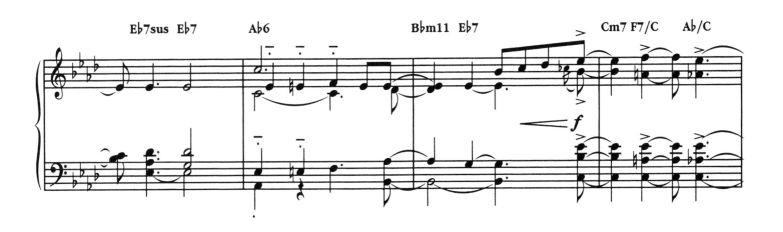

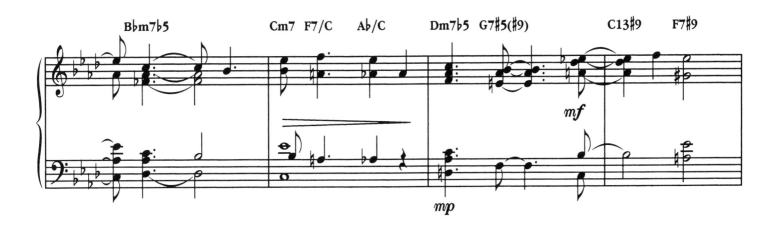

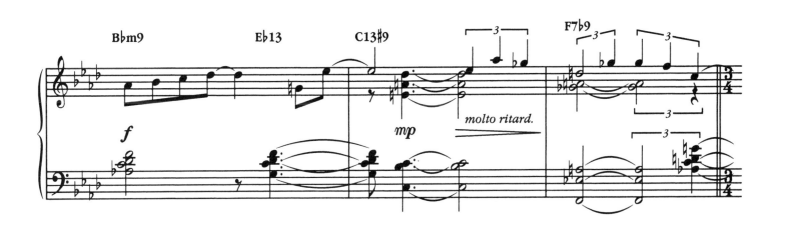

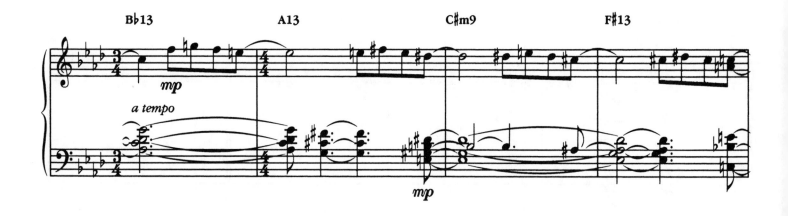

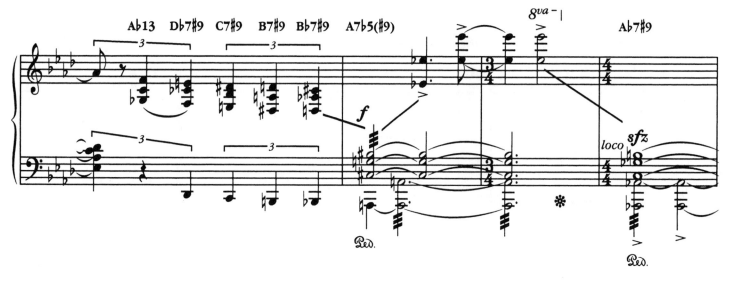

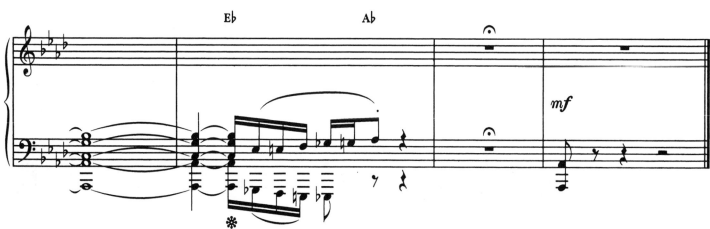

If I Were a Bell

from *GUYS AND DOLLS*

By Frank Loesser

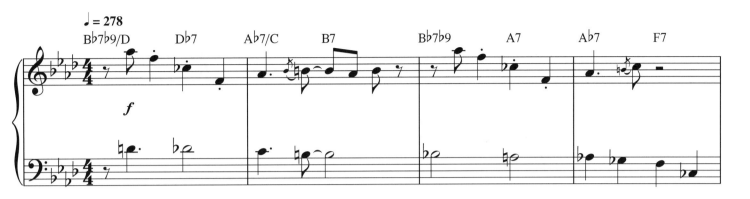

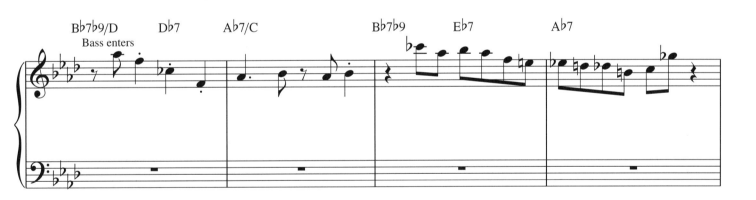

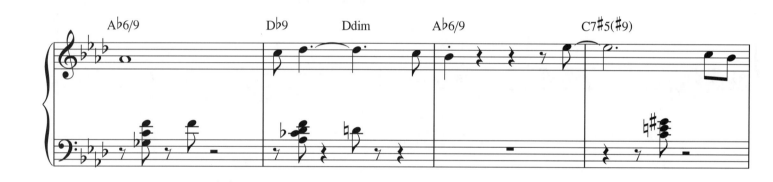

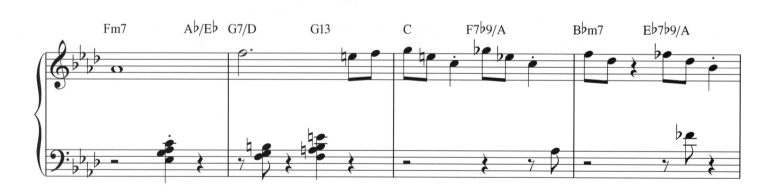

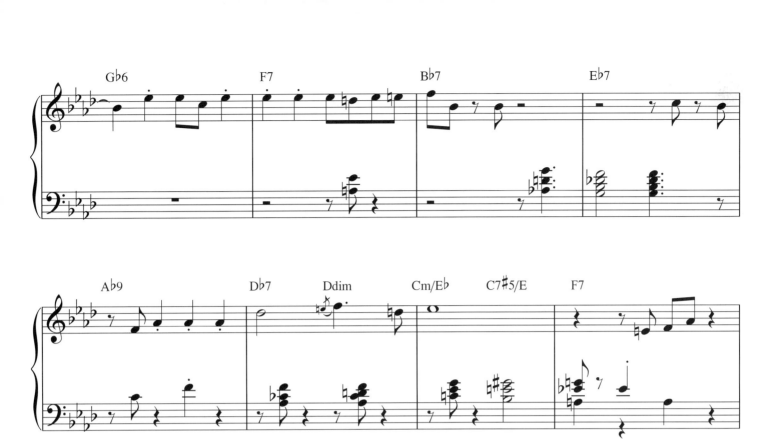

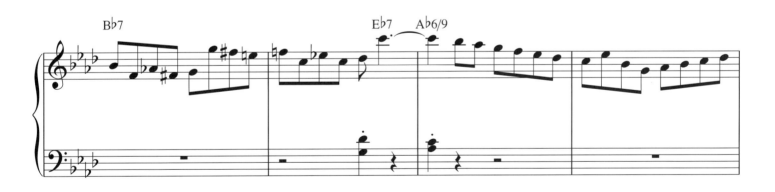

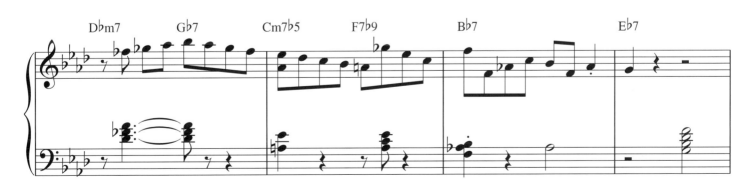

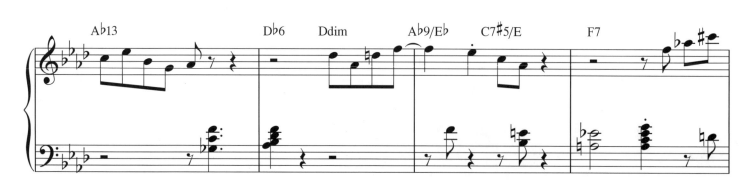

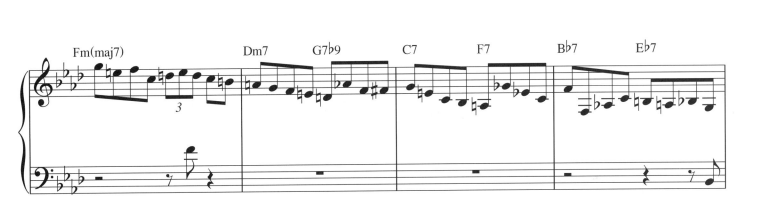

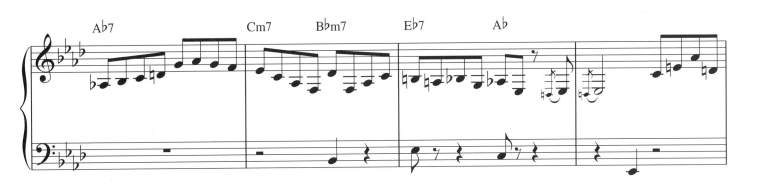

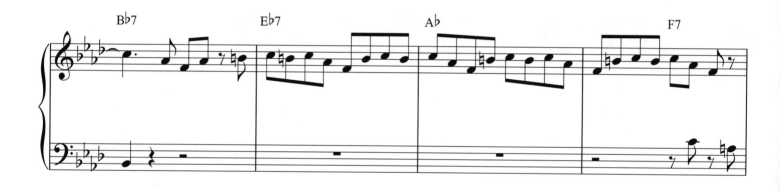

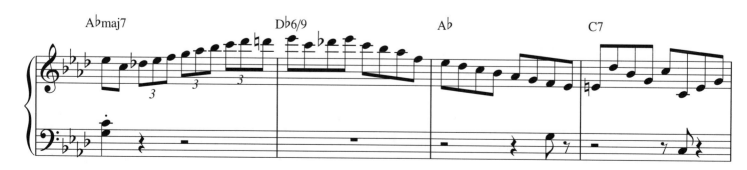

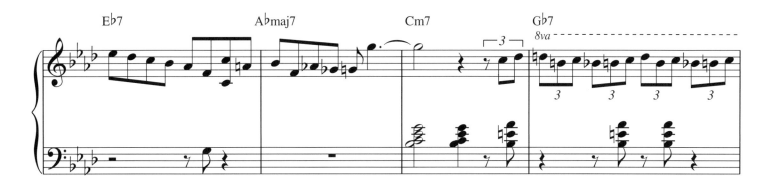

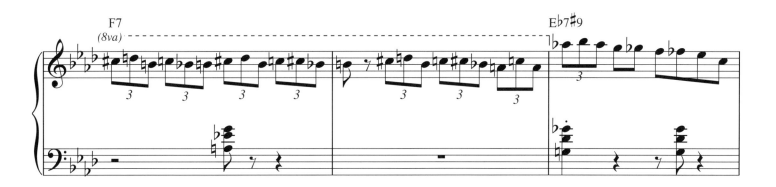

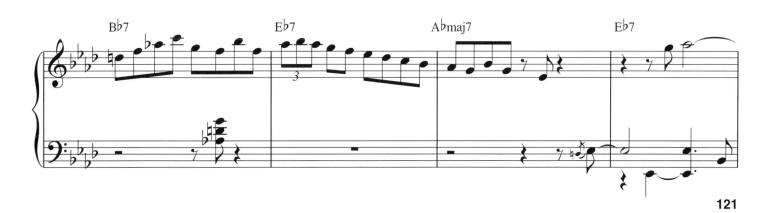

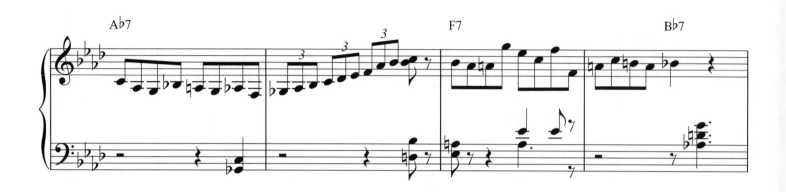

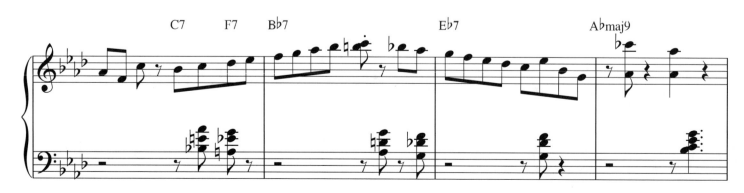

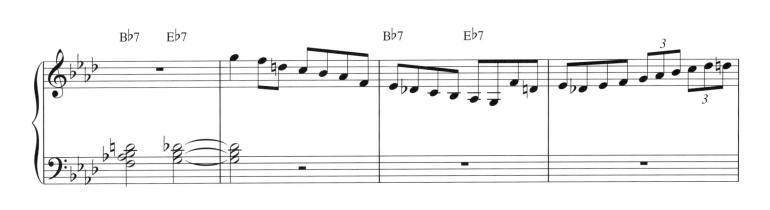

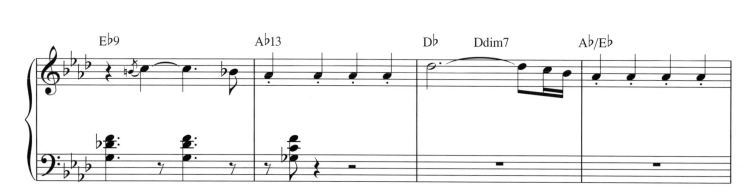

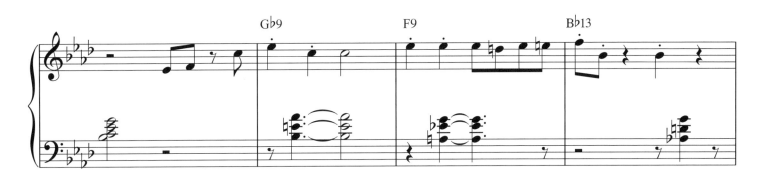

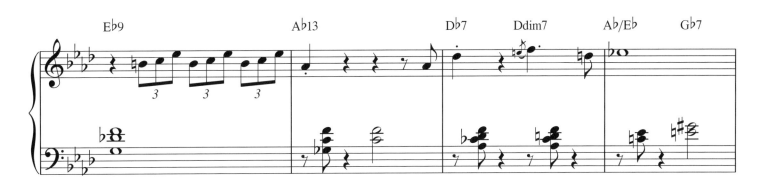

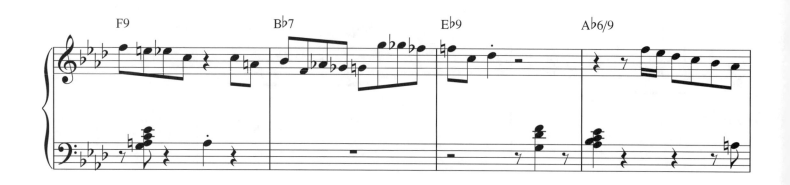

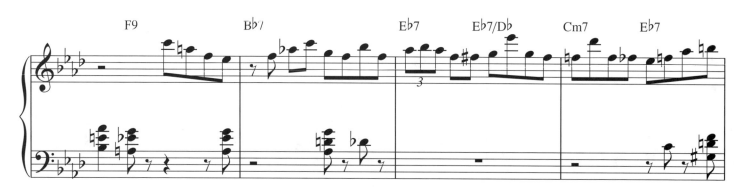

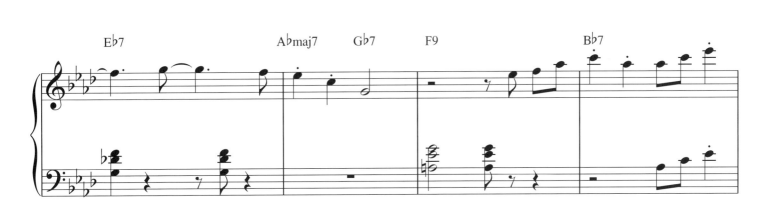

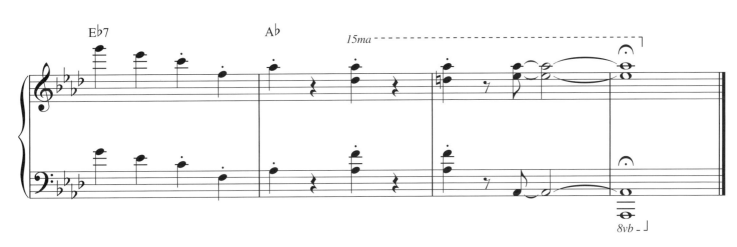

In a Sentimental Mood
By Duke Ellington

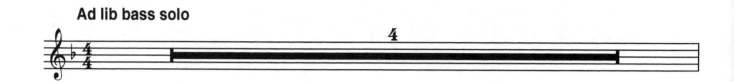

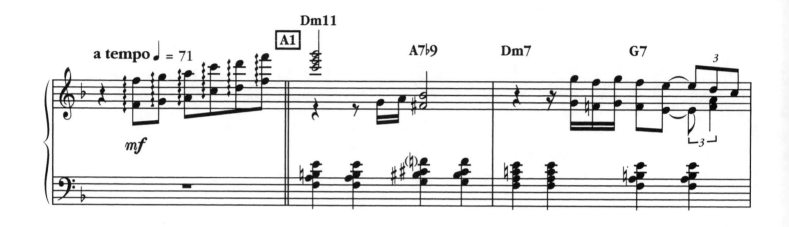

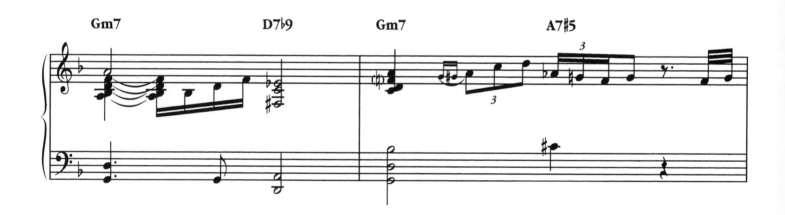

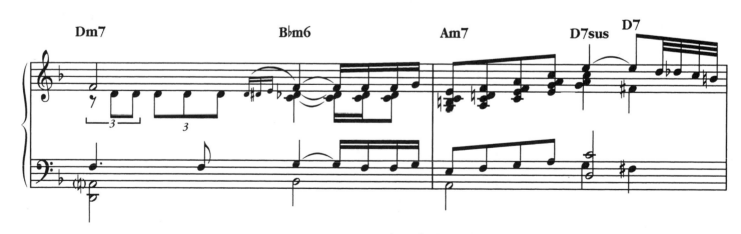

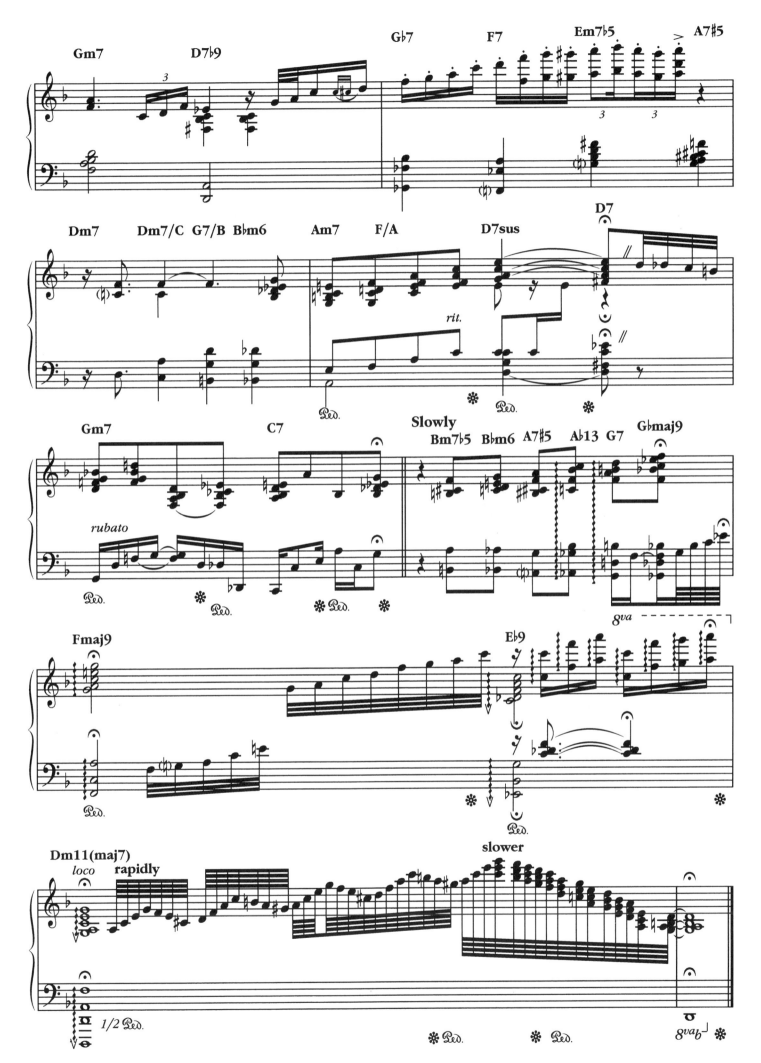

King Porter Stomp

By Ferd "Jelly Roll" Morton

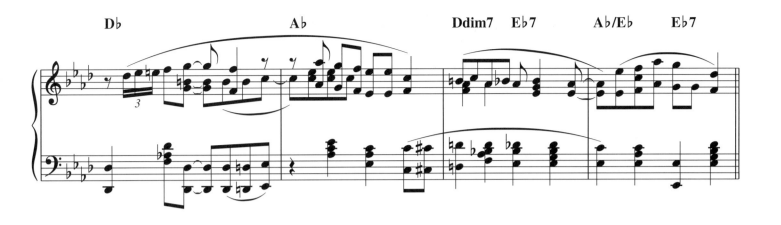

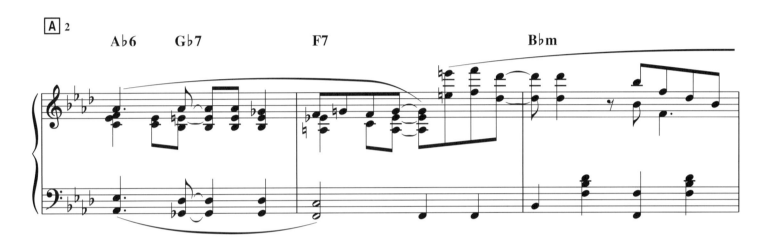

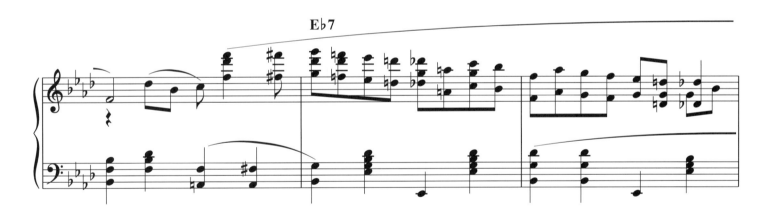

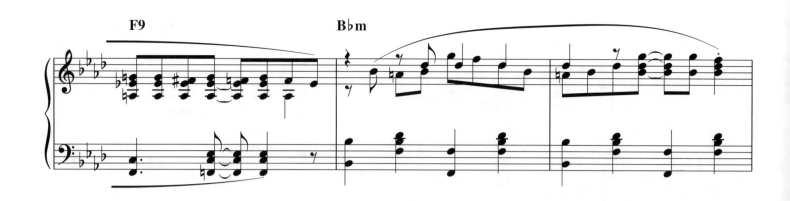

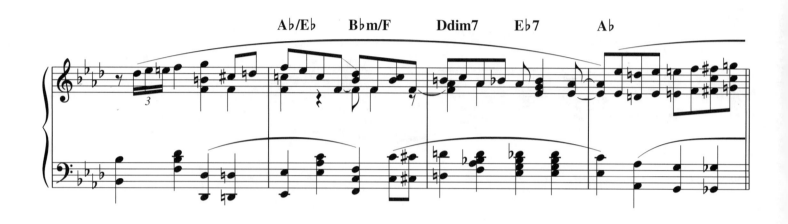

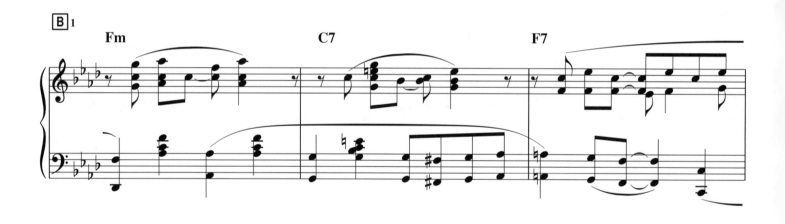

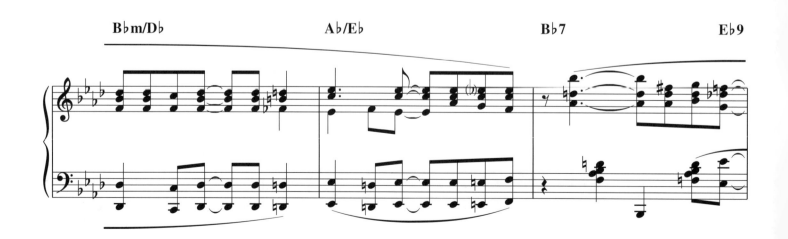

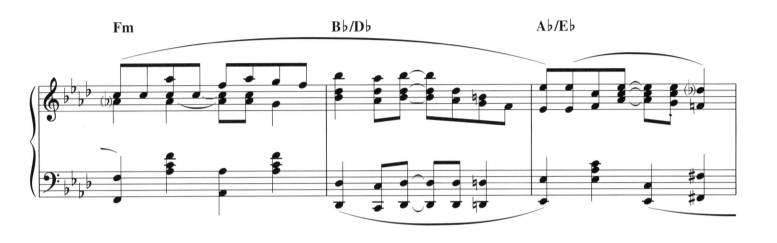

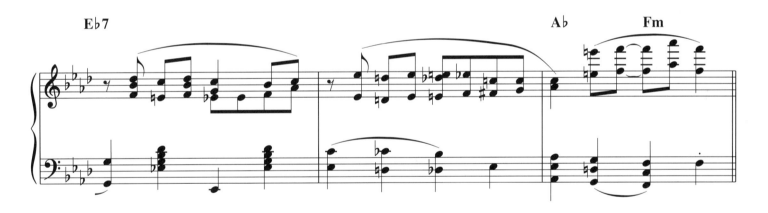

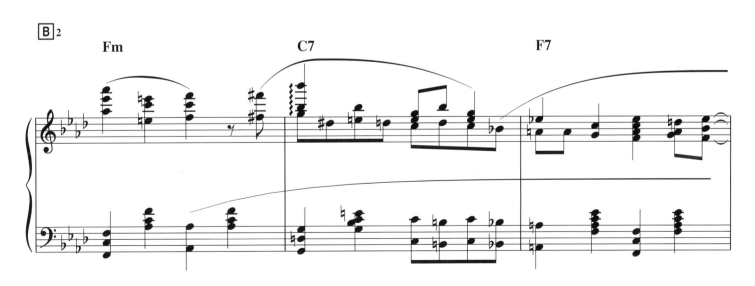

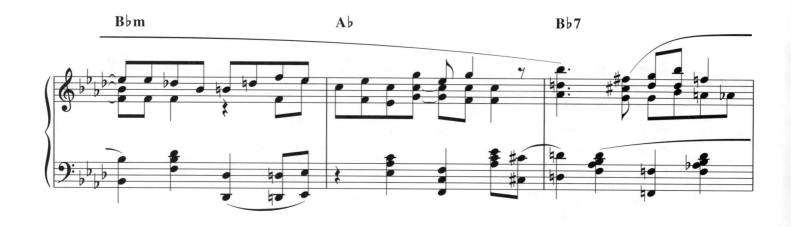

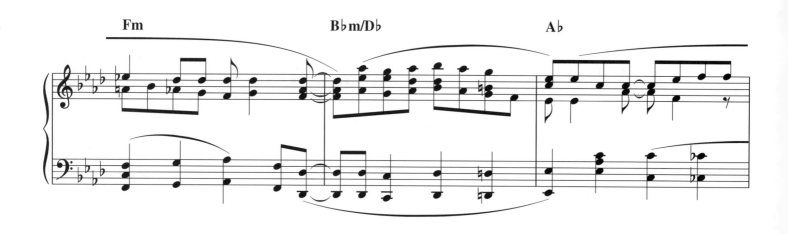

Long Ago
(And Far Away)
from *COVER GIRL*

Words by Ira Gershwin
Music by Jerome Kern

152

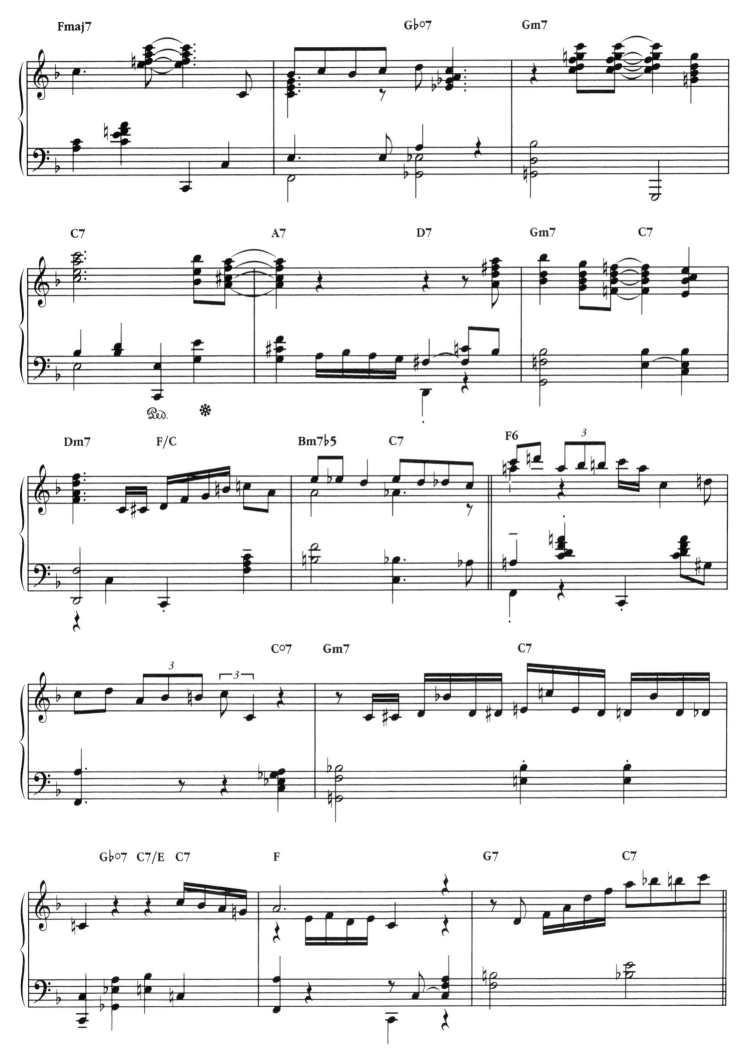

A Night in Tunisia

By John "Dizzy" Gillespie and Frank Paparelli

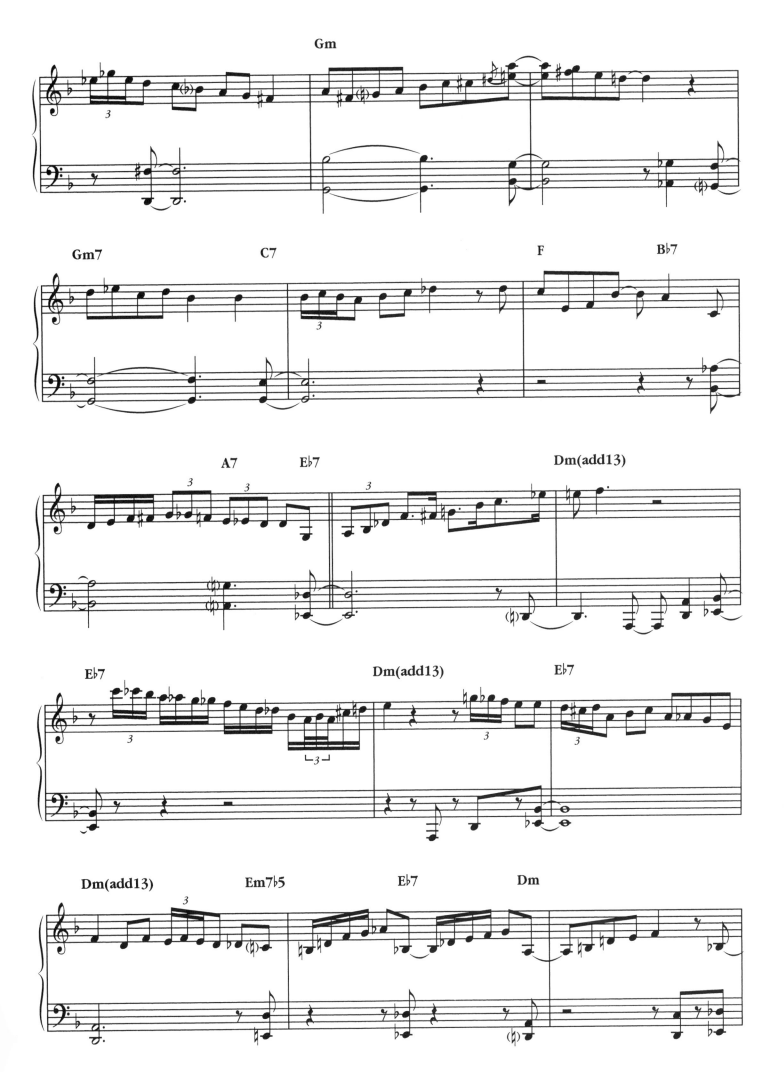

No Moon at All

By Dave Mann and Redd Evans

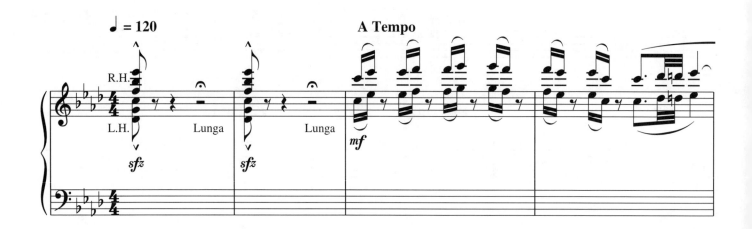

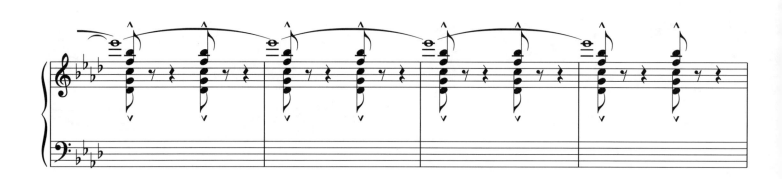

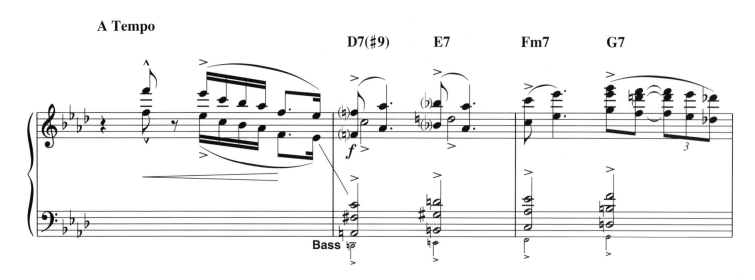

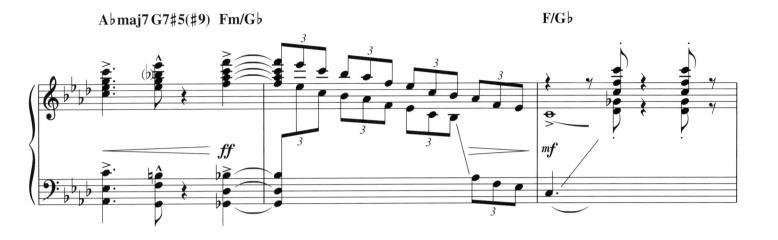

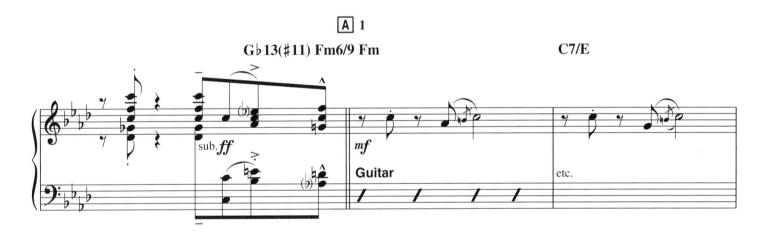

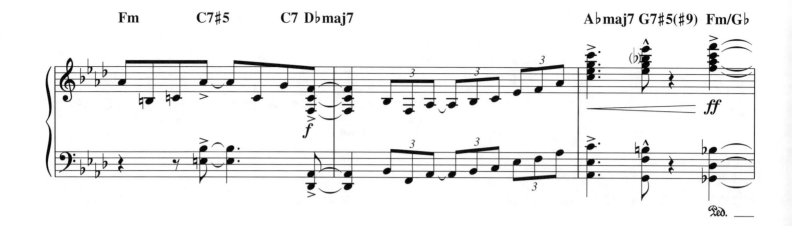

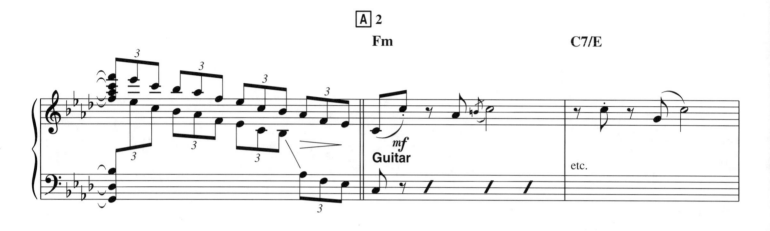

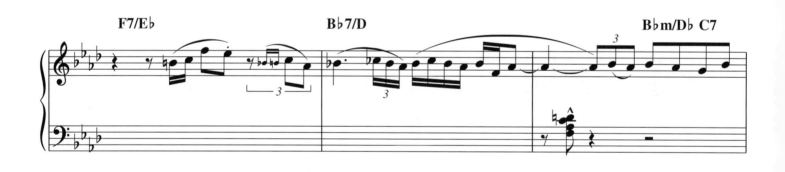

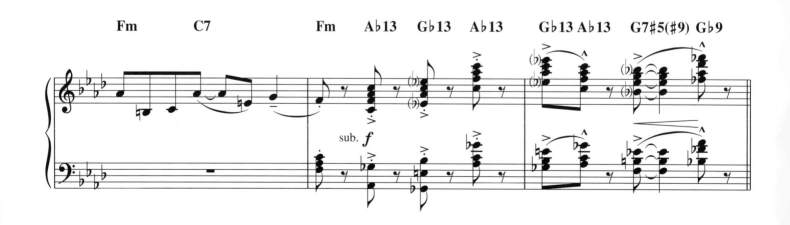

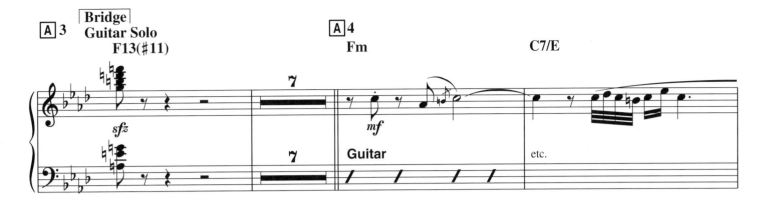

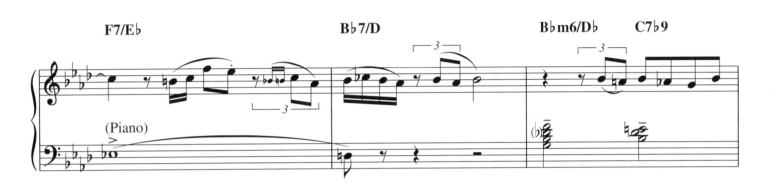

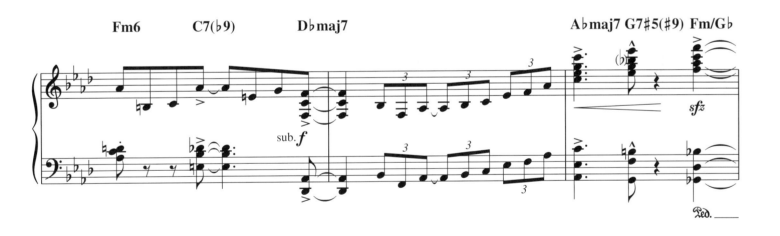

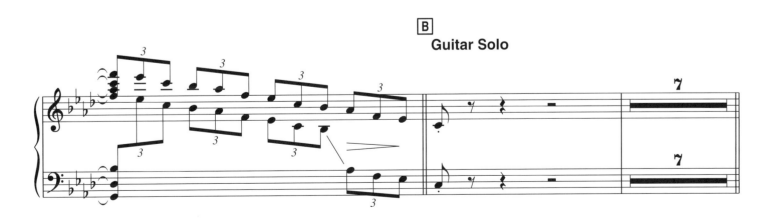

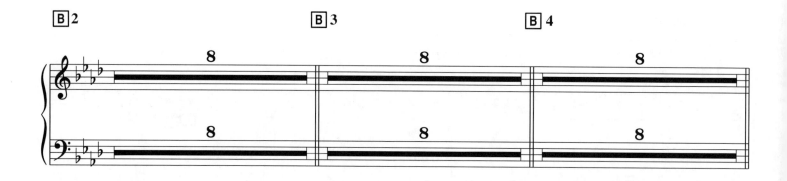

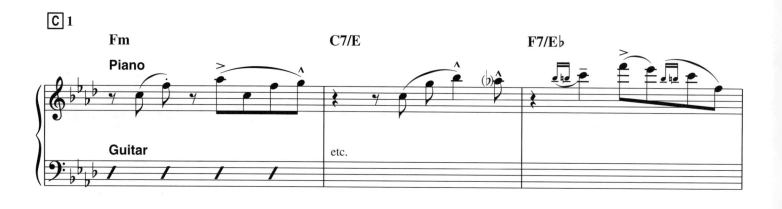

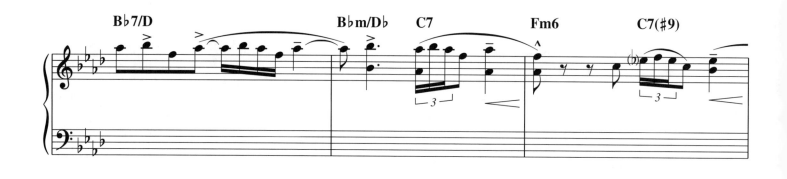

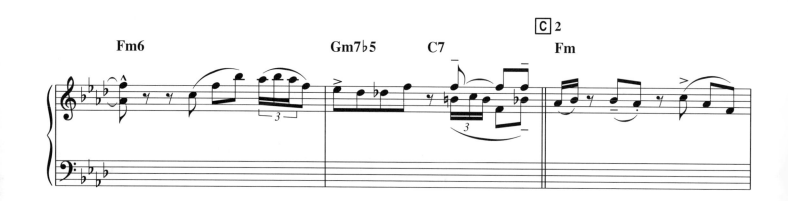

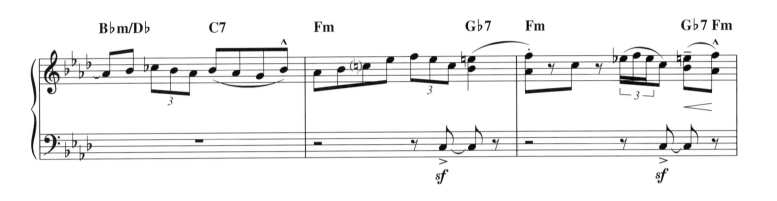

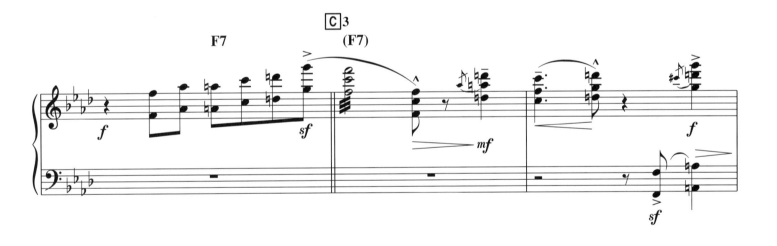

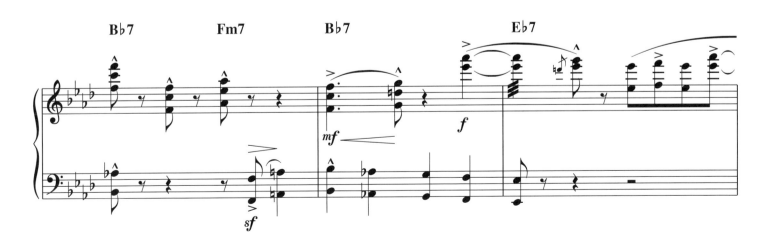

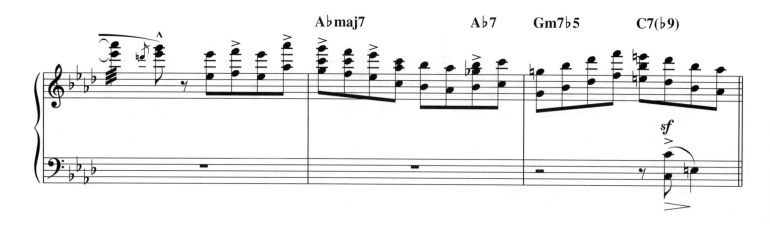

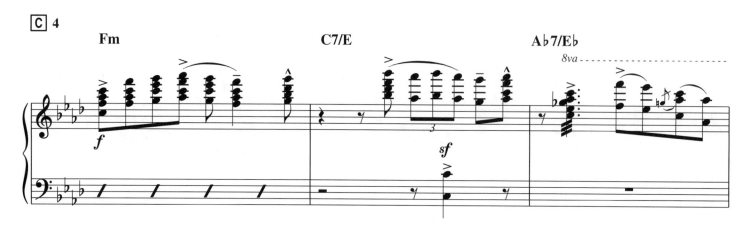

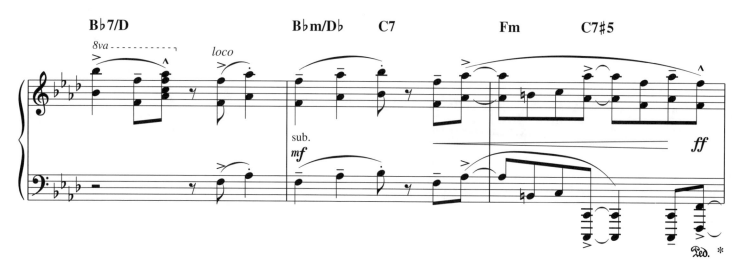

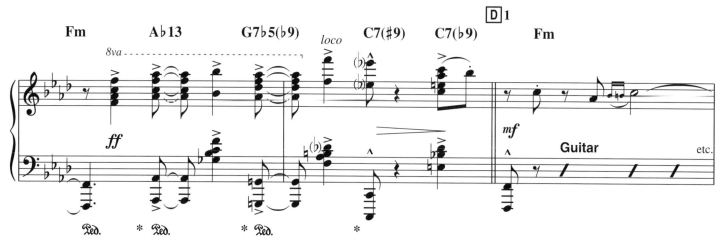

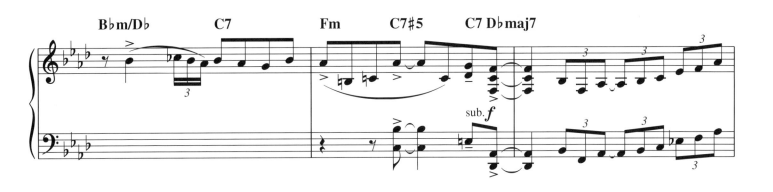

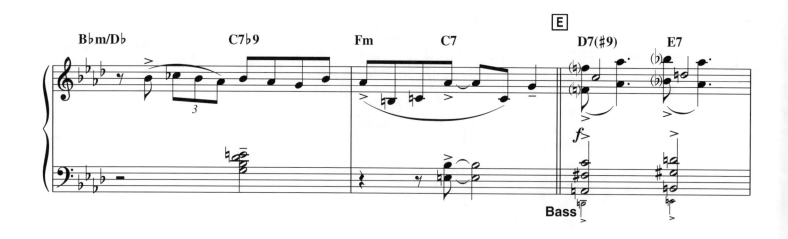

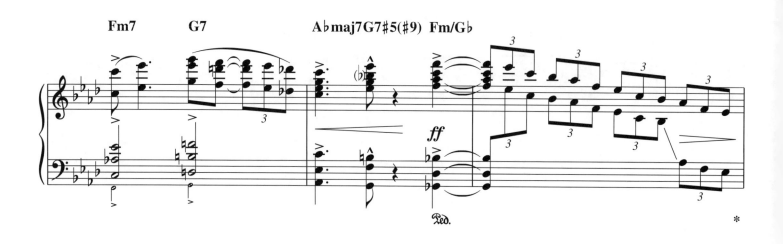

Stormy Weather
(Keeps Rainin' All the Time)
from *COTTON CLUB PARADE OF 1933*

Lyric by Ted Koehler
Music by Harold Arlen

On the Sunny Side of the Street

Lyric by Dorothy Fields
Music by Jimmy McHugh

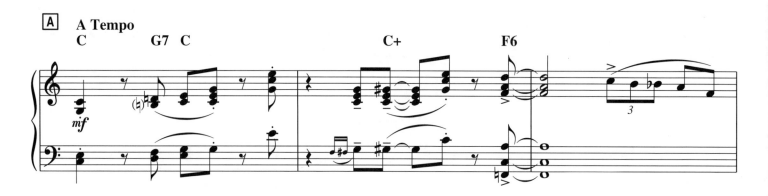

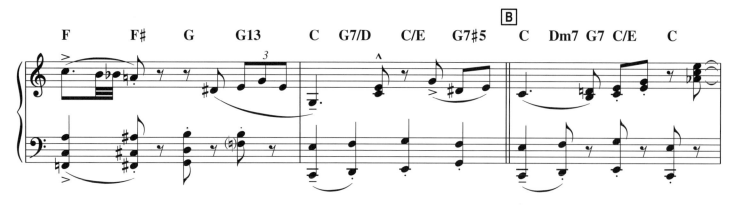

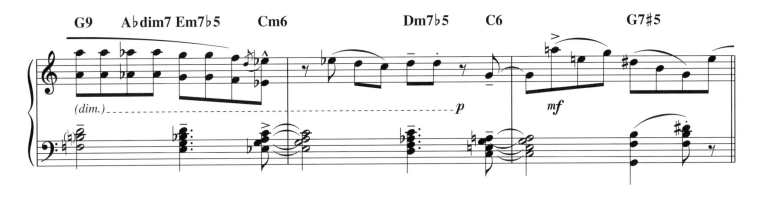

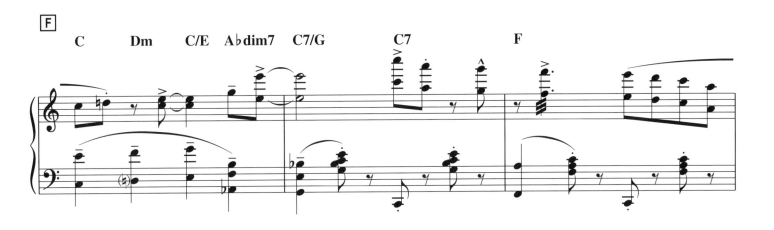

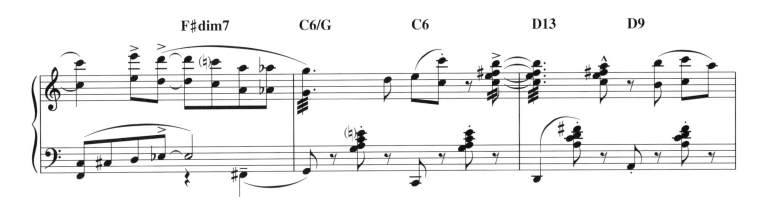

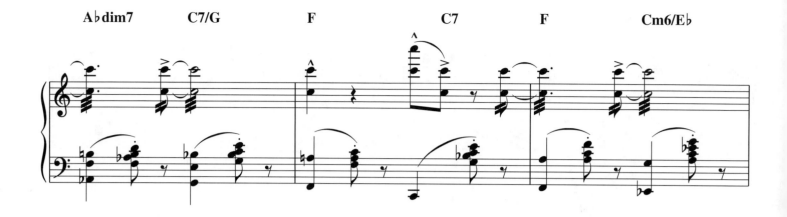

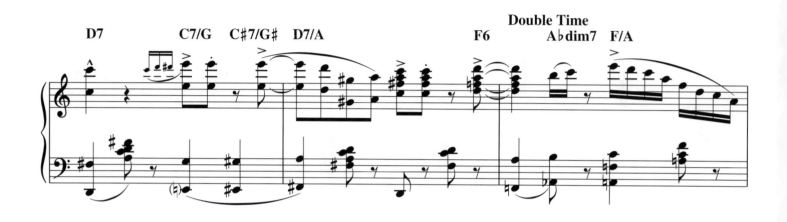

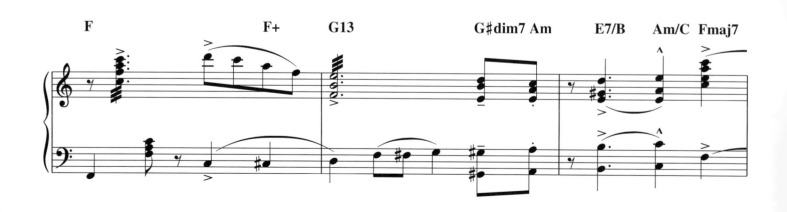

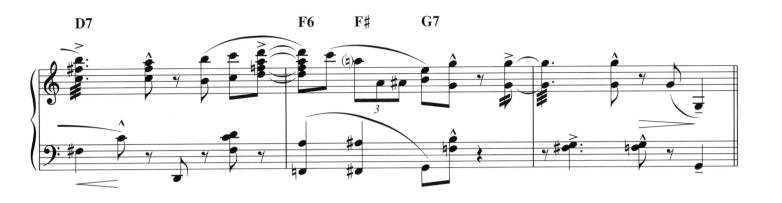

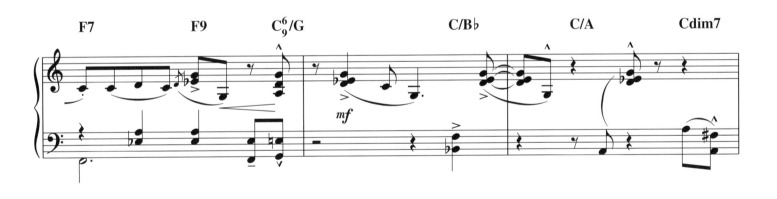

The Single Petal of a Rose
from *QUEEN'S SUITE*
By Duke Ellington

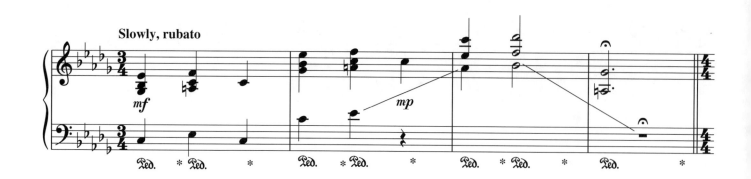

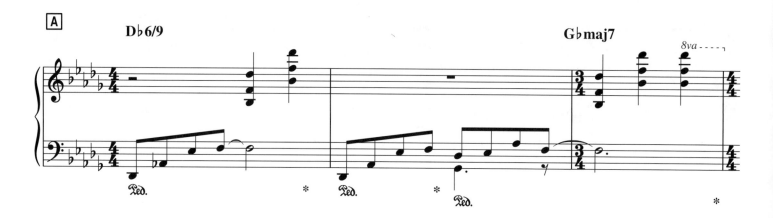

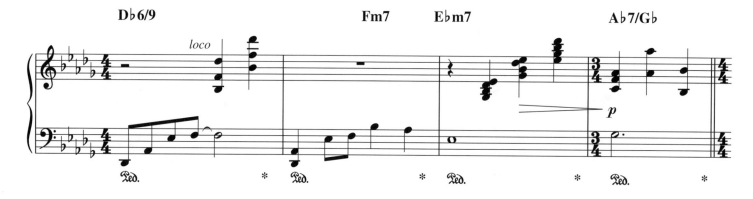

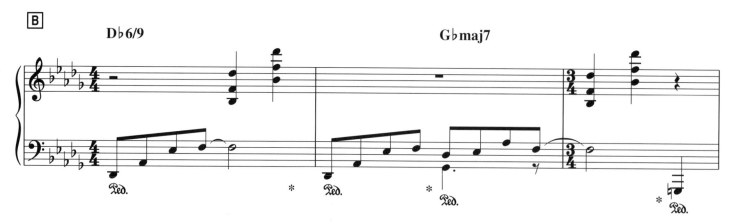

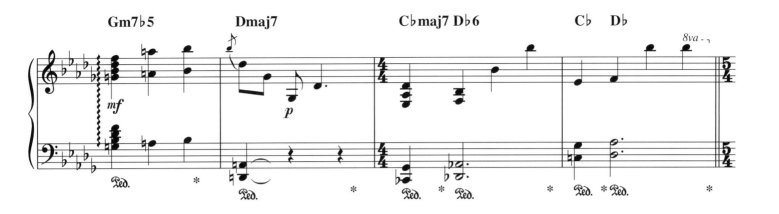

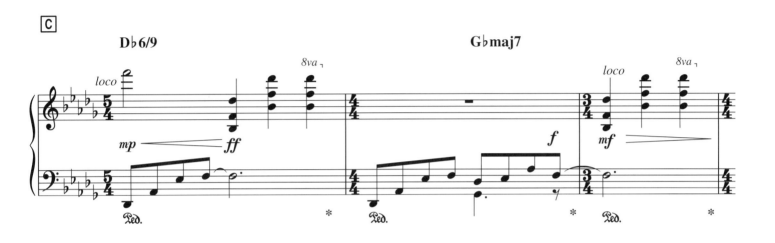

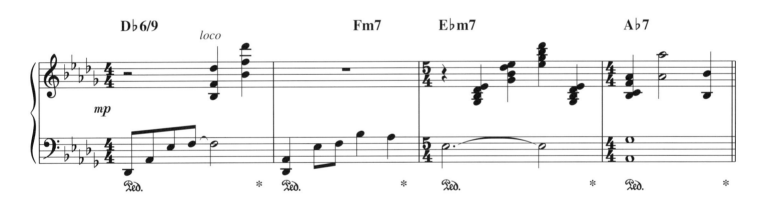

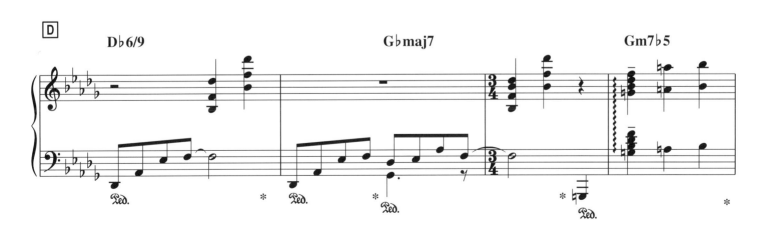

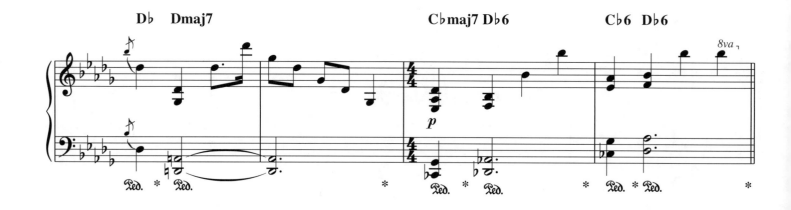

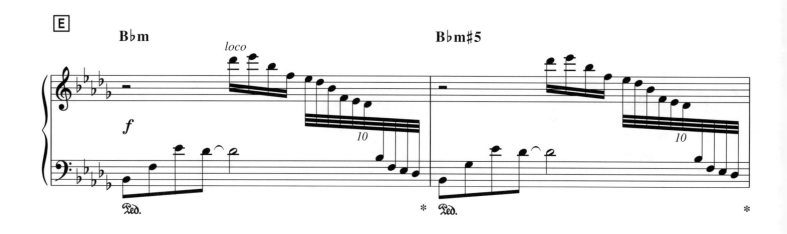

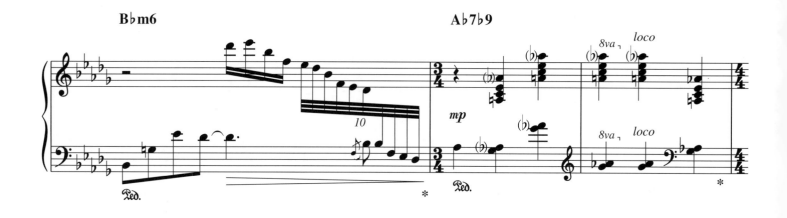

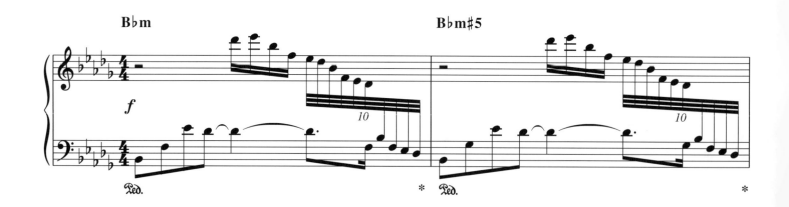

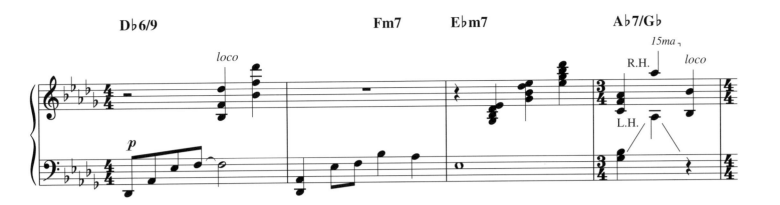

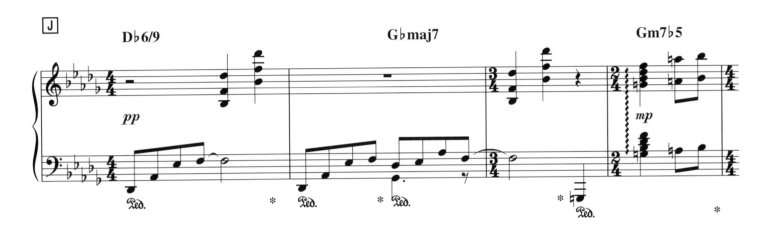

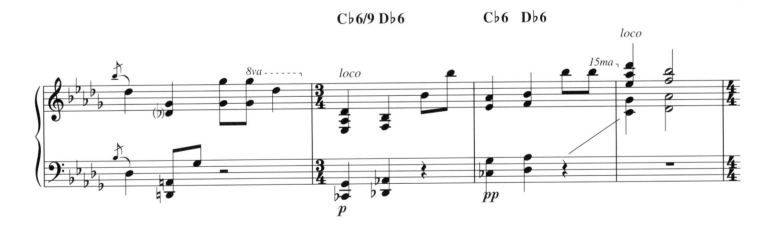

Why Do I Love You?

from *SHOW BOAT*

Lyrics by Oscar Hammerstein II
Music by Jerome Kern

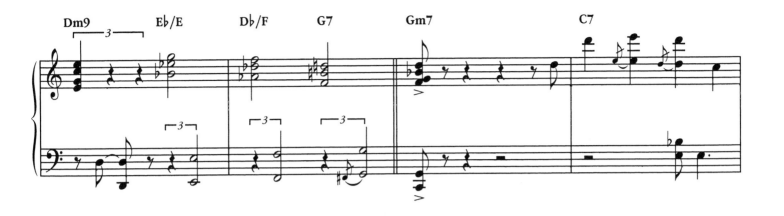

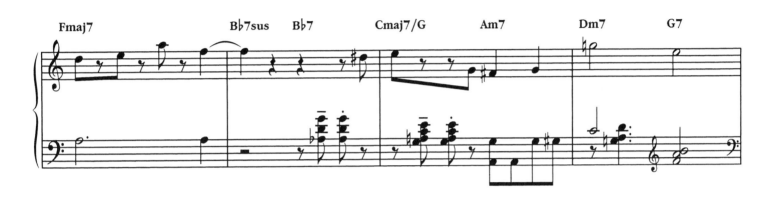

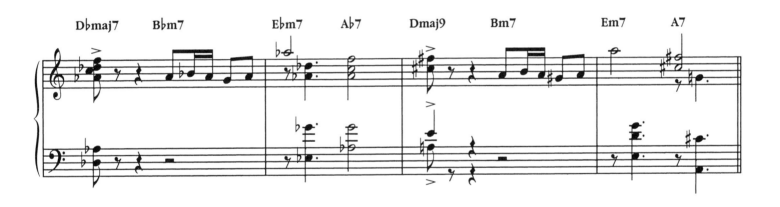

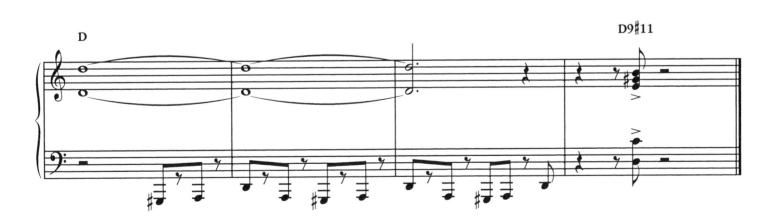

Where or When

from *BABES IN ARMS*

Words by Lorenz Hart
Music by Richard Rodgers

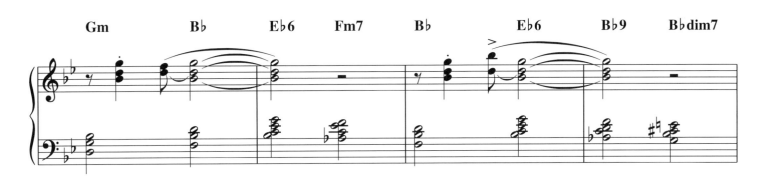

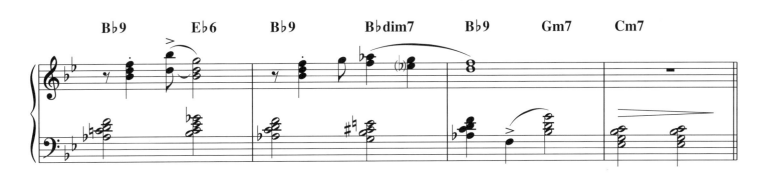

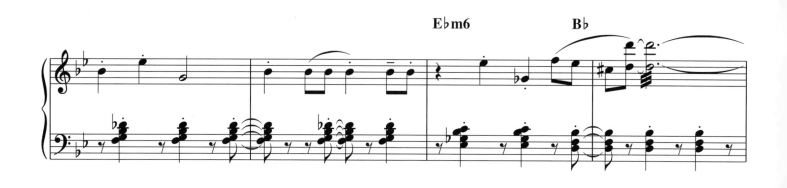

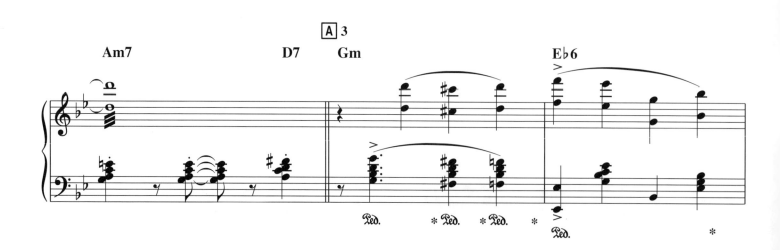

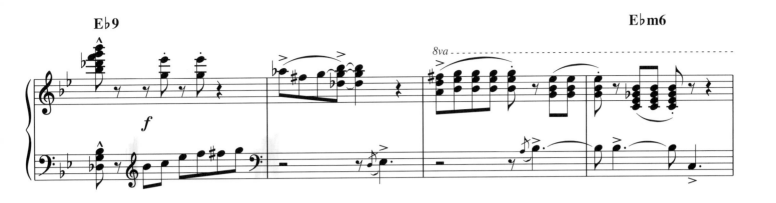

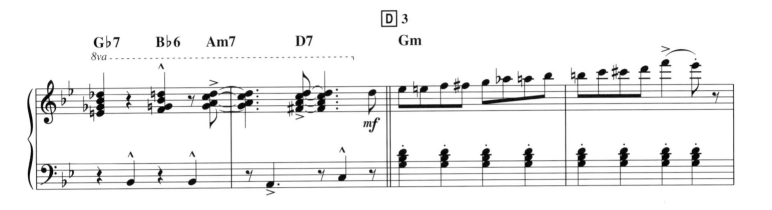

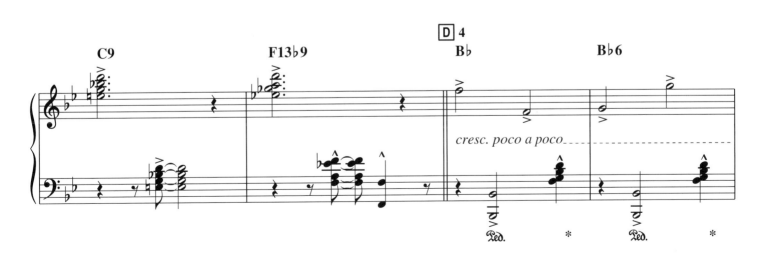

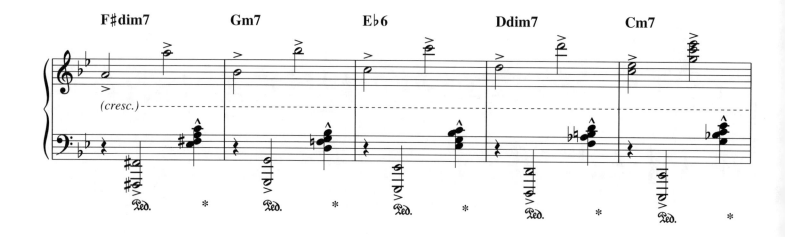

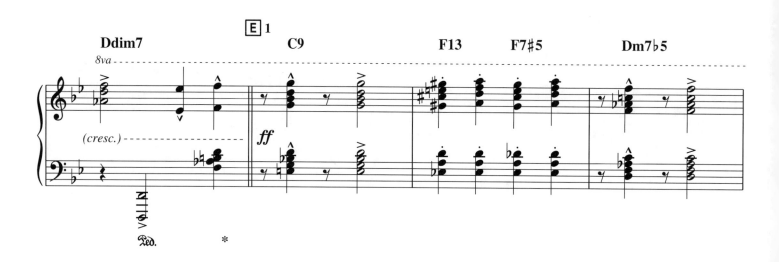

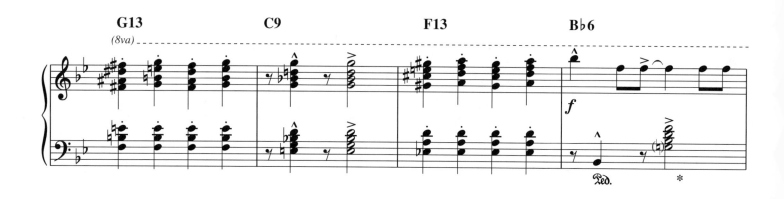

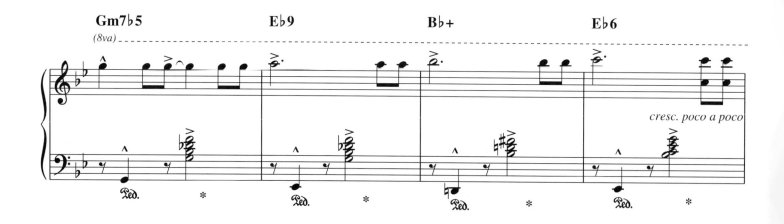

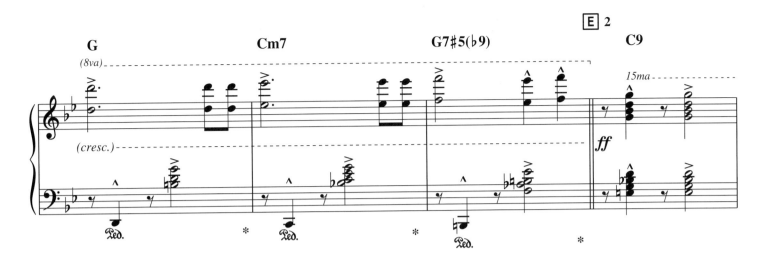

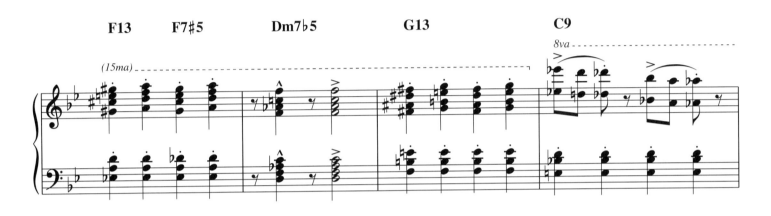

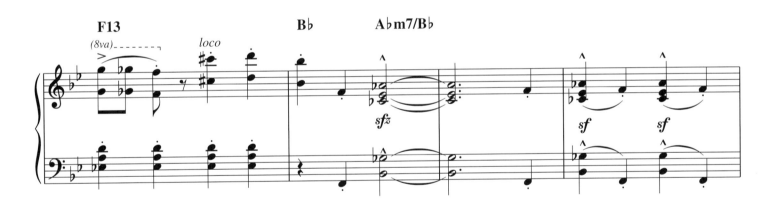

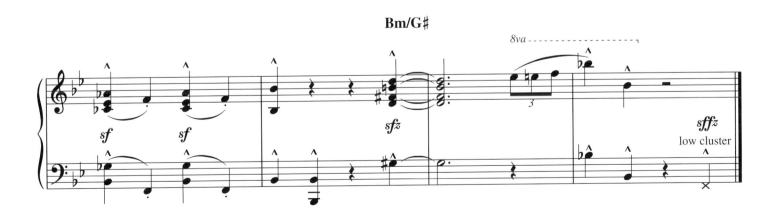

The Surrey with the Fringe on Top

from *OKLAHOMA!*

Lyrics by Oscar Hammerstein II
Music by Richard Rodgers

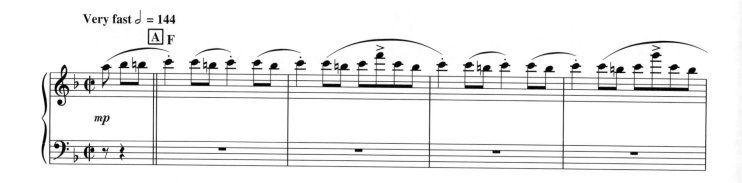

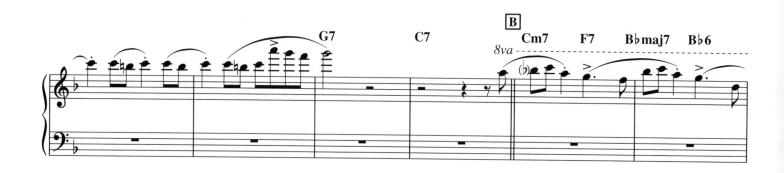

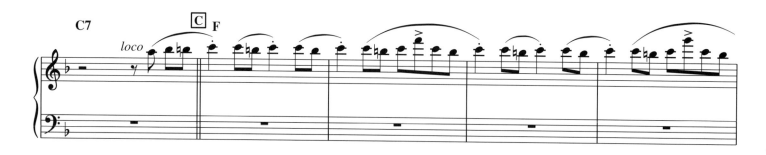

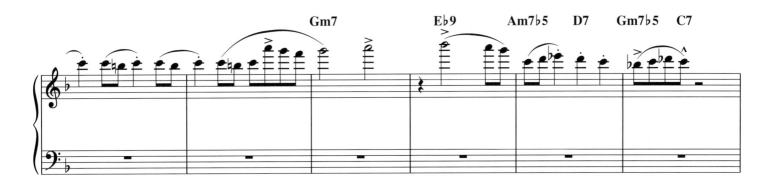

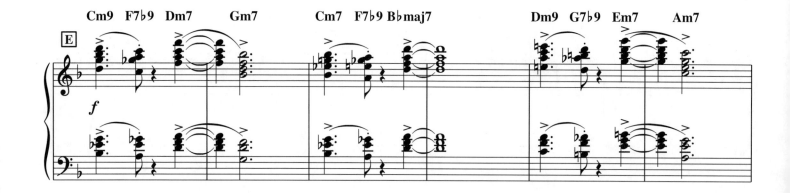

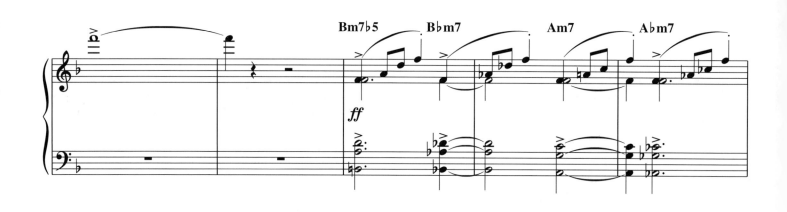

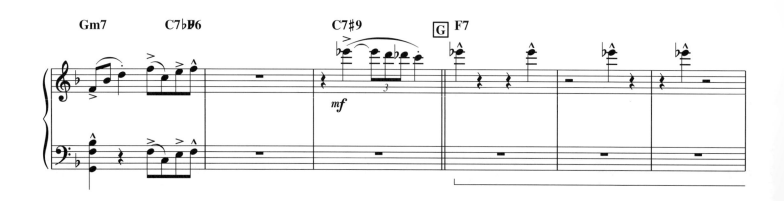

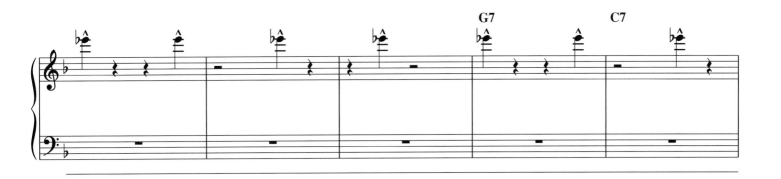

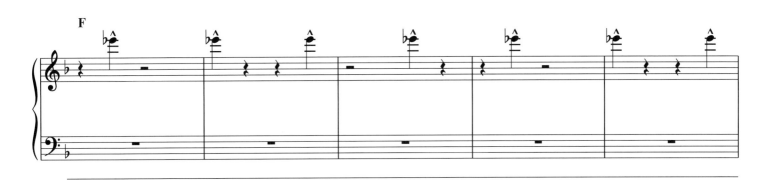

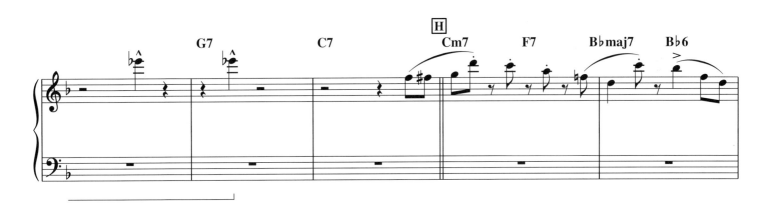

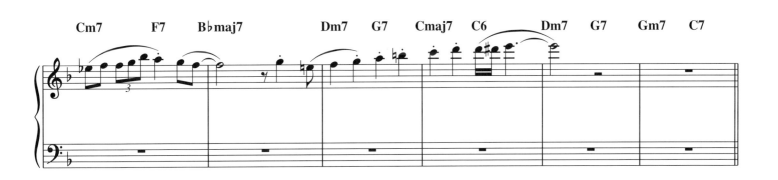

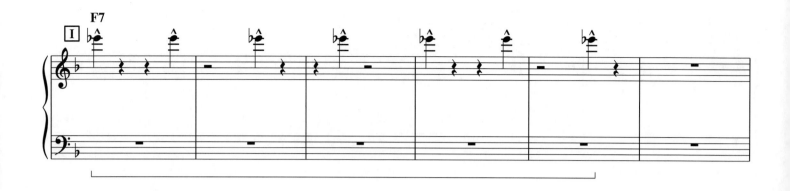

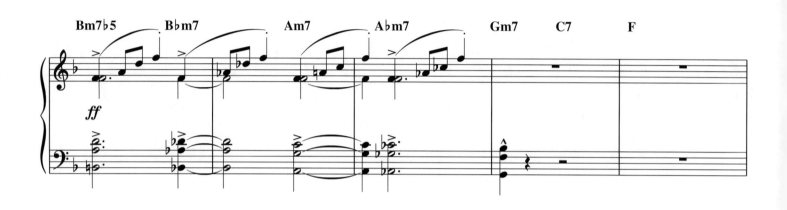

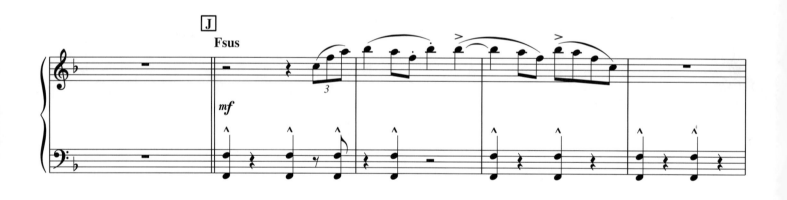

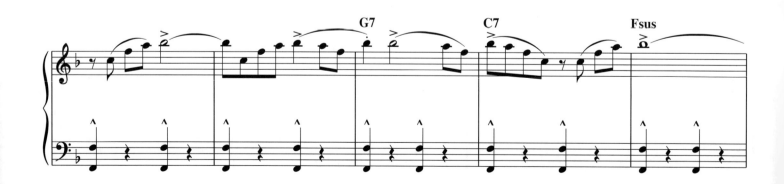

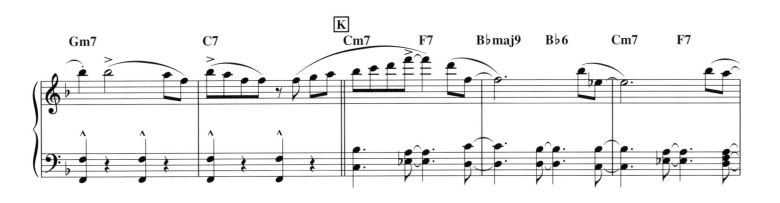

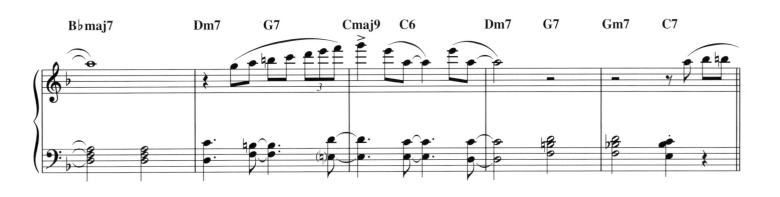

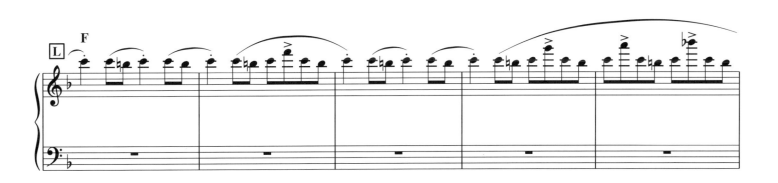

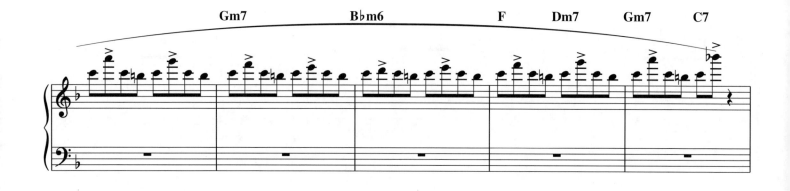

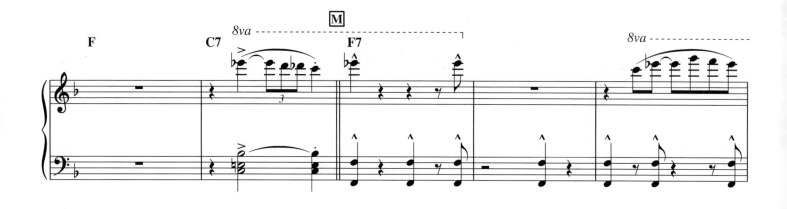

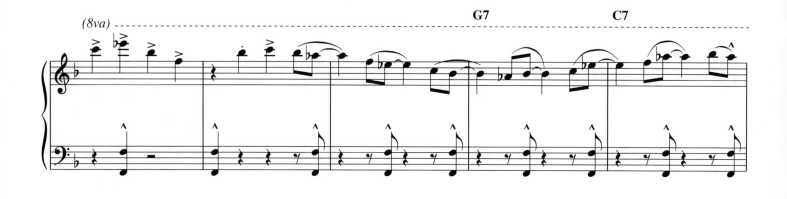

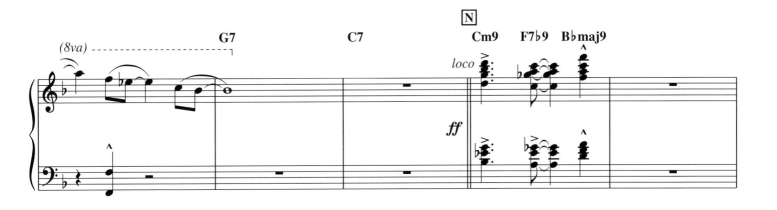

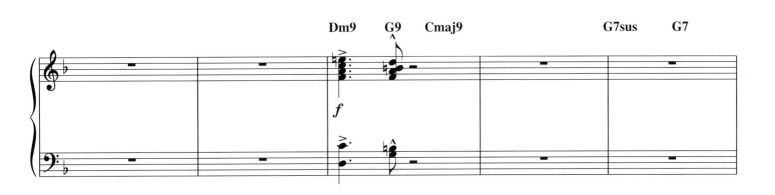

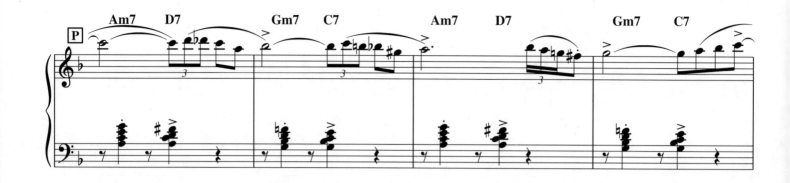

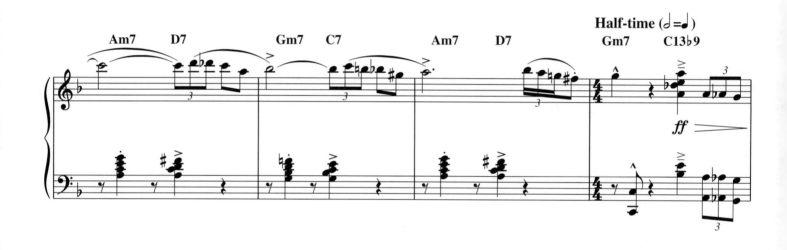